THE
HARPERCOLLINS
BIBLE PRONUNCIATION GUIDE

THE HARPERCOLLINS BIBLE PRONUNCIATION GUIDE

GENERAL EDITOR

William O. Walker, Jr.

ASSOCIATE EDITORS
Toni Craven
J. Andrew Dearman

With the Society of Biblical Literature

HarperSanFrancisco
A Division of HarperCollins*Publishers*

FIRST HARPERCOLLINS PAPERBACK EDITION PUBLISHED IN 1994

ISBN 0-06-068962-5 (pbk)

An Earlier Edition of This Book Was Cataloged As Follows:

Harper's Bible pronunciation guide / general editor, William O. Walker, Jr. : associate editors, Toni Craven, J. Andrew Dearman with the Society of Biblical Literature.
    p. cm.
    ISBN 0-06-068951-X (cloth)
    1. Names in the Bible—Pronunciation. 2. Bible—Terminology—Pronunciation. I. Walker, William O., Jr. II. Craven, Toni. III. Dearman, John Andrew. IV. Society of Biblical Literature.
BS435.H35   1989
220.5′2′0014—dc19   89-45241
                                                      CIP

        02 03 HAD 11

This edition is printed on acid-free paper and meets the American National Standards Institute Z39.48 Standard.

CONTENTS

PREFACE

WILLIAM O. WALKER, JR.

The goal of this book is to provide a simple and easily understandable guide for the pronunciation of every proper name in the English Bible (including the Apocrypha), certain other biblical terms that may be unfamiliar to some readers and not readily accessible in most general dictionaries, and a number of technical and other terms that are important for biblical study but do not appear in the biblical texts. The work is divided into two sections: "Biblical Terms" (both proper and common names) and "Nonbiblical Terms."

So that no appropriate biblical term would inadvertently be omitted and that the guide could be used with as many English translations of the Bible as possible, the editors have consulted all of the available concordances,[1] as well as such works as *The Interpreter's Dictionary of the Bible*,[2] *Harper's Bible Dictionary*,[3] *The Eerdmans Bible Dictionary*,[4] W. Murray Severance's *Pronouncing Bible Names*,[5] and *Webster's New Twentieth Century Dictionary of the English Language*.[6] They have also checked a number of specific names in various Bible translations for which no concordance was available.[7] In compiling the list of nonbiblical terms, reference was made not only to the dictionaries already cited but also to the indices in numerous introductions to the Bible and to the Old and New Testaments.

Somewhat arbitrary decisions made by the editors include the following: (1) Even where the plural form occurs in the biblical texts (and sometimes only the plural), only the singular is included for English words and, in most cases, for Anglicized forms of foreign words. (2) Separate listings are included for different spellings of the same term, even where the difference involves only hyphenation or word division. (3) In the section devoted to biblical terms, words that serve as both proper and common names are listed separately, even if the pronunciations are the same (capitalized words are proper names, and noncapitalized ones are common names). (4) Terms that appear in "Biblical Terms" are not repeated in "Nonbiblical Terms," even when they refer to a different subject.

The most difficult problem in compiling a Bible pronunciation guide is, of course, that of determining the correct pronunciation for each of the terms included. More than half a century ago, John D. Davis summarized the situation regarding the pronunciation of biblical names as follows:

> The pronunciation of anglicized Scripture proper names is still in a chaotic state. In the majority of names the syllabification and accentuation have never been settled. Even the systems of pronunciation most in vogue are unnecessarily

inconsistent. A chief reason for this is that the pronunciation has been so largely based on the forms which the Greek and Latin translators gave to the Hebrew names. These translators did not transliterate the names in accordance with any fixed rule; and, as a result, names of similar formation and pronunciation in Hebrew appear in different forms in the Greek and Latin; and often, when quite similar in appearance in English, retain the divergent Greek or Latin pronunciation. In many cases this is intolerable.[8]

Davis's observations are still more or less true.

It is generally agreed that "proper pronunciation is determined by current usage."[9] In many cases, such usage is clear and consistent; thus, wherever possible, this rule is to be followed. Often, however, current usage is difficult if not impossible to determine. For some biblical terms, two or more different pronunciations are commonly used (e.g., ab'uh and ah'buh for "Abba"). Moreover, there is sometimes a serious discrepancy between pronunciations used by scholars and those found in more popular usage (e.g., bah'ahl and bay'uhl for "Baal"). In addition, "large numbers of biblical names are spoken only rarely, so that no established usage can be found for them."[10] The matter is further complicated, as Davis noted, by the fact that the forms in which many biblical terms now appear in English "are the results of passage through several languages [e.g., Greek and Latin] with their own distinctive patterns of pronunciation."[11] Thus, "it is impossible to say what is 'correct' pronunciation of many biblical terms, especially of names from the Old Testament."[12]

In this work, the following principles are applied regarding the pronunciation of biblical terms: (1) Where current usage is clear and consistent, it is followed. (2) In most cases, only one pronunciation is given for each term. (3) In a few cases where there are significant differences among scholars, between scholars and the general public, and/or within the public, alternative pronunciations are given; in such cases, the pronunciation judged more "popular" by the editors is given first. (4) In other cases where differences in pronunciation exist, the pronunciation given is the one that is, in the judgment of the editors, most widely used and/or most nearly consistent with the pronunciation of other terms having similar English spellings. (5) Whenever possible, pronunciations most familiar to the English-speaking tongue are preferred over those that are less familiar. (6) Where biblical names are also used as personal names today, the contemporary pronunciations are given unless a different biblical pronunciation is well established.

The editors would not claim that the pronunciations given are, in every case, the only or even necessarily the best pronunciations; they do believe, however, that each pronunciation given is an acceptable and defensible one. It is their hope that this work may contribute toward standardizing the pronunciation of biblical terms in the English-speaking world.

At only one point during this project have the editors confronted a problem of moral principle. This regarded the inclusion of such gender-specific terms as "Canaanitess," "Moabitess," and the like (note also the translation "deaconess" in Romans 16:1). Objecting in principle to the use of such terminology (one of the editors commented, "I am an American, not an Americaness!"), they nevertheless concluded that the terms must be included because the original goal of the work had been to list every proper name in the various English translations of the Bible.

Obviously, this pronunciation guide could never have been completed without the dedicated and conscientious work of the general editor's two associate editors, Toni Craven and J. Andrew Dearman; it has been a genuine pleasure and privilege for the general editor to work with them. The Society of Biblical Literature, under whose aegis this work has been prepared, has been most helpful; particular appreciation is extended to Gene M. Tucker, the Chair of SBL's Research and Publications Committee, and Kent Harold Richards, the Society's Executive Secretary when the project began. Finally, John B. Shopp and Kandace Hawkinson at Harper & Row have, from the very beginning, been both encouraging and supportive, have provided welcome advice and counsel, and have been exceedingly patient with delays in the completion of the project.

It is the sincere hope of the editors that this pronunciation guide will make it easier for both scholars and ordinary readers of the biblical texts to understand what they read and to enter imaginatively into the world of the biblical writers and their original readers.

NOTES

1. James Strong, *The Exhaustive Concordance of the Bible: Showing Every Word of the Text of the Common English Version of the Canonical Books, and Every Occurrence of Each Word in Regular Order; Together with a Key-Word Comparison of Selected Words and Phrases in the King James Version with Five Leading Contemporary Translations; Also Brief Dictionaries of the Hebrew and Greek Words of the Original, with References to the English Words* (Nashville, TN: Abingdon, 1890, 1980); John W. Ellison, *Nelson's Complete Concordance of the Revised Standard Version Bible*, 2d ed. (Nashville, TN, Camden, NJ, and New York: Thomas Nelson, 1984); Bible Data Bank of the Centre Informatique et Bible (Abbey of Maredsous), *A Concordance to the Apocrypha/Deuterocanonical Books of the Revised Standard Version* (Grand Rapids, MI: Eerdmans, London: Collins, 1983); Stephen J. Hartdegen, general ed., *Nelson's Complete Concordance of the New American Bible* (Nashville, TN, and New York: Thomas Nelson, 1977); *The Complete Concordance to the Bible: New King James Version* (Nashville, TN, Camden, NJ, and New York: Thomas Nelson, 1983); Edward W. Goodrick and John R. Kohlenberger, III, *The NIV Complete Concordance: The Complete English Concordance to the New International Version* (Regency Reference Library; Grand Rapids, MI: Zondervan, 1981); and Robert L. Thomas, general ed., *New American Standard Exhaustive Concordance of the Bible: Hebrew-Aramaic and Greek Dictionaries* (Nashville, TN: Holman, 1981).
2. George Arthur Buttrick et al., eds., *The Interpreter's Dictionary of the Bible: An Illustrated Encyclopedia Identifying and Explaining All Proper Names and Significant Terms and Subjects in the Holy Scriptures, Including the Apocrypha, with Attention to Archaeological Discoveries and Researches into the Life and Faith of Ancient Times*, 4 vols. (New York and Nashville, TN: Abingdon, 1962); and Keith Crim et al., eds., *ibid.*, supplementary vol. (Nashville, TN: Abingdon, 1976).
3. Paul J. Achtemeier et al., eds., *Harper's Bible Dictionary* (San Francisco: Harper & Row, 1985).
4. Allen C. Myers et al., eds., *The Eerdmans Bible Dictionary* (Grand Rapids, MI: Eerdmans, 1987).
5. W. Murray Severance, *Pronouncing Bible Names*, rev. ed. (Nashville, TN: Holman, 1985).
6. Jean L. McKechnie et al., eds., *Webster's New Twentieth Century Dictionary of the English Language: Unabridged*, 2d ed. (London : Collins, 1980), esp. pp. 86–99 of Supplements.

7. For example, J. B. Phillips, *The New Testament in Modern English* (New York: Macmillan, 1962); *The New English Bible with the Apocrypha* (Oxford: Oxford University Press and Cambridge: Cambridge University Press, 1970); Henry Wansbrough, general ed., *The New Jerusalem Bible* (Garden City, NY: Doubleday, 1985); and *Tanakh: A New Translation of the Holy Scriptures According to the Traditional Hebrew Text* (Philadelphia, New York, and Jerusalem: The Jewish Publications Society, 1985).

8. John D. Davis, *A Dictionary of the Bible*, 4th ed. (Grand Rapids, MI: Baker, 1924), p. iv.

9. Buttrick et al., eds., *Interpreter's Dictionary of the Bible*, 1:xxvii.

10. Ibid.

11. Geoffrey W. Bromiley et al., eds., *The International Standard Bible Encyclopedia*, rev. ed. (Grand Rapids, MI: Eerdmans, 1979–), 1:viii.

12. Ibid.

PRONUNCIATION KEY

a	cat	ihr	**ear**	ou	how
ah	father	j	joke	p	pat
ahr	lard	k	king	r	run
air	care	kh	**ch** as in Ger-	s	so
aw	jaw		man *Buch*	sh	sure
ay	pay	ks	vex	t	toe
b	bug	kw	quill	th	thin
ch	chew	l	love	*th*	then
d	do	m	mat	ts	tsetse
e, eh	pet	n	not	tw	twin
ee	seem	ng	sing	uh	ago
er	error	o	hot	uhr	her
f	fun	oh	go	v	vow
g	good	oi	boy	w	weather
h	hot	oo	foot	y	young
hw	whether	*oo*	boot	z	zone
i	it	oor	poor	zh	vision
i	sky	or	for		

Stress accents are printed after stressed syllables:

   ' primary stress
   , secondary stress

THE HARPERCOLLINS BIBLE PRONUNCIATION GUIDE

BIBLICAL TERMS

A

Aalar	ay'uh-luhr
Aaron	air'uhn
Aaronic	air-on'ik
Aaronite	air'uh-n*i*t
Abacuc	ab'uh-kuhk
Abaddon	uh-bad'uhn
Abadias	ab'uh-d*i*'uhs
Abagtha	uh-bag'thuh
Abana	ab'uh-nuh
Abanah	ab'uh-nuh
Abarim	ab'uh-rim
Abba	ah'buh, ab'uh
Abbas	ah'buhs
Abda	ab'duh
Abdeel	ab'dee-uhl
Abdenago	ab-den'uh-goh
Abdi	ab'd*i*
Abdias	ab-d*i*'uhs
Abdiel	ab'dee-uhl
Abdon	ab'duhn
Abednego	uh-bed'ni-goh
Abed-nego	uh-bed'ni-goh
Abel	ay'buhl
Abelbethmaacah	ay'buhl-beth-may'uh-kuh
Abel-beth-maacah	ay'buhl-beth-may'uh-kuh
Abel Bethmaacah	ay'buhl-beth-may'uh-kuh
Abel Beth Maacah	ay'buhl-beth-may'uh-kuh
Abel-beth-maachah	ay'buhl-beth-may'uh-kuh
Abel Beth Maachah	ay'buhl-beth-may'uh-kuh
Abelkeramim	ay'buhl-ker'uh-mim
Abel-keramim	ay'buhl-ker'uh-mim
Abel Keramim	ay'buhl-ker'uh-mim
Abelmaim	ay'buhl-may'im

Abel-maim	ay'buhl-may'im
Abel Maim	ay'buhl-may'im
Abelmeholah	ay'buhl-mi-hoh'luh
Abel-meholah	ay'buhl-mi-hoh'luh
Abel Meholah	ay'buhl-mi-hoh'luh
Abelmizraim	ay'buhl-miz'ray-im
Abel-mizraim	ay'buhl-miz'ray-im
Abel Mizraim	ay'buhl-miz'ray-im
Abelshittim	ay'buhl-shit'im
Abel-shittim	ay'buhl-shit'im
Abel Shittim	ay'buhl-shit'im
Abez	ay'bez
Abi	ay'b*i*
Abia	uh-b*i*'uh
Abiah	uh-b*i*'uh
Abialbon	ay'b*i*-al'buhn
Abi-albon	ay'b*i*-al'buhn
Abiasaph	uh-b*i*'uh-saf
Abiathar	uh-b*i*'uh-thahr
Abib	ay'bib
Abibaal	ay'b*i*-bay'uhl
Abida	uh-b*i*'duh
Abidah	uh-b*i*'duh
Abidan	uh-b*i*'duhn
Abiel	ay'bee-uhl
Abiezer	ay'b*i*-ee'zuhr
Abi-ezer	ay'b*i*-ee'zuhr
Abiezrite	ay'b*i*-ez'r*i*t
Abi-ezrite	ay'b*i*-ez'r*i*t
Abigail	ab'uh-gayl
Abigal	ab'uh-gal
Abihail	ab'uh-hayl
Abihu	uh-b*i*'hy*oo*
Abihud	uh-b*i*'huhd
Abijah	uh-b*i*'juh
Abijam	uh-b*i*'juhm
Abilene	ab'uh-lee'nee
Abimael	uh-bim'ay-uhl
Abimelech	uh-bim'uh-lek
Abinadab	uh-bin'uh-dab
Abiner	ab'uh-nuhr
Abinoam	uh-bin'oh-uhm
Abiram	uh-b*i*'ruhm
Abisei	ab'uh-see'*i*
Abishag	ab'uh-shag

---

a cat, ah father, ahr lard, air care, aw jaw, ay pay, b bug, ch chew, d do,
e, eh pet, ee seem, er error, f fun, g good, h hot, hw whether, i it, *i* sky,
ihr ear, j joke, k king, kh ch as in German *Buch*, ks vex, kw quill, l love, m mat,

Abishai	uh-b*i*′sh*i*
Abishalom	uh-bish′uh-luhm
Abishua	uh-bish′*oo*-uh
Abishur	uh-b*i*′shuhr
Abisum	uh-b*i*′suhm
Abital	uh-b*i*′tuhl
Abitub	uh-b*i*′tuhb
Abiud	uh-b*i*′uhd
Abner	ab′nuhr
Abraham	ay′bruh-ham
Abram	ay′bruhm
abrek	ay′brek
Abron	ay′bruhn
Abronah	uh-broh′nuh
Absalom	ab′suh-luhm
Abshai	ab′sh*i*
Abubus	uh-b*oo*′buhs
abyss	uh-bis′
Acacia	uh-kay′shuh
Acatan	ak′uh-tan
Acbor	ak′bor
Accad	ak′ad
Accaron	ak′uh-ruhn
Accho	ak′oh
Acco	ak′oh
Accos	ak′oz
Accoz	ak′oz
Aceldama	uh-kel′duh-muh
Achab	ay′kab
Achaia	uh-kay′yuh
Achaicus	uh-kay′uh-kuhs
Achan	ay′kan
Achar	ay′kahr
Achaz	ay′kaz
Achbor	ak′bohr
Achiacharus	ak′yuh-kay′ruhs
Achias	uh-k*i*′uhs
Achim	ay′kim
Achimelech	uh-kim′uh-lek
Achior	ay′kee-ohr
Achish	ay′kish
Achitob	ak′uh-tob
Achmetha	ak′muh-thuh
Achor	ay′kohr
Achsa	ak′suh

---

n **n**ot, ng si**ng**, o h**o**t, oh g**o**, oi b**oy**, oo f**oo**t, *oo* b**oo**t, oor p**oor**, or f**or**,
ou h**ow**, p **p**at, r **r**un, s **s**o, sh **s**ure, t **t**oe, th **th**in, *th* **th**en, ts **ts**etse,
tw **tw**in, uh **a**go, uhr h**er**, v **v**ow, w **w**eather, y **y**oung, z **z**one, zh vi**s**ion

Achsah	ak'suh
Achshaph	ak'shaf
Achzib	ak'zib
Acipha	uh-s*i*'fuh
Acitho	as'uh-thoh
Acraba	ak'ruh-buh
Acrabbim	uh-krab'im
acropolis	uh-krop'uh-lis
Acsah	ak'suh
Acshaph	ak'shaf
Acts	akts
Acua	uh-kyoo'uh
Acub	ay'kuhb
Aczib	ak'zib
Adadah	ad'uh-duh
Adah	ay'duh
Adaiah	uh-day'yuh
Adalia	uh-day'lee-uh
Adam	ad'uhm
Adamah	ad'uh-muh
Adami	ad'uh-m*i*
Adaminekeb	ad'uh-m*i*-nee'keb
Adami-nekeb	ad'uh-m*i*-nee'keb
Adami Nekeb	ad'uh-m*i*-nee'keb
Adan	ay'duhn
Adar	ay'dahr
Adasa	ad'uh-suh
Adbeel	ad'bee-uhl
Addan	ad'uhn
Addar	ad'ahr
Addi	ad'*i*
Addo	ad'oh
Addon	ad'uhn
Addus	ad'uhs
Ader	ay'duhr
Adida	ad'uh-duh
Adiel	ay'dee-uhl
Adin	ay'din
Adina	ad'uh-nuh
Adino	ad'uh-noh
Adinus	uh-d*i*'nuhs
Adithaim	ad'uh-thay'im
Adlai	ad'l*i*
Admah	ad'muh
Admatha	ad-may'thuh

a cat, ah father, ahr lard, air care, aw jaw, ay pay, b bug, ch chew, d do,
e, eh pet, ee seem, er error, f fun, g good, h hot, hw whether, i it, *i* sky,
ihr ear, j joke, k king, kh ch as in German Buch, ks vex, kw quill, l love, m mat,

Admin	ad'min
Adna	ad'nuh
Adnah	ad'nuh
Adonai	ad'oh-n*i*'
Adonay	ad'oh-n*i*'
Adonibezek	uh-doh'n*i*-bee'zek
Adoni-bezek	uh-doh'n*i*-bee'zek
Adonijah	ad'uh-n*i*'juh
Adonikam	ad'uh-n*i*'kuhm
Adoniram	ad'uh-n*i*'ruhm
Adonizedek	uh-doh'n*i*-zee'dek
Adoni-zedek	uh-doh'n*i*-zee'dek
Adora	uh-doh'ruh
Adoraim	ad'-uh-ray'im
Adoram	uh-doh'ruhm
Adrammelech	uh-dram'uh-lek
Adramyttian	ad'ruh-mit'ee-uhn
Adramyttium	ad'ruh-mit'ee-uhm
Adria	ay'dree-uh
Adriatic	ay'dree-a'tik
Adriel	ay'dree-uhl
Aduel	uh-dy*oo*'uhl
Adullam	uh-duhl'uhm
Adullamite	uh-duhl'uh-m*i*t
Adummim	uh-duhm'im
Aeneas	i-nee'uhs
Aenon	ee'nuhn
Aesora	i-soh'ruh
Agaba	ag'uh-buh
Agabus	ag'uh-buhs
Agade	uh-gah'dee
Agag	ay'gag
Agagite	ay'guh-g*i*t
Agar	ay'gahr
Agee	ay'gee
Aggaeus	ag'ee-uhs
Aggeus	ag'ee-uhs
Agia	ay'gee-uh
Agrippa	uh-grip'uh
Agur	ay'guhr
Ahab	ay'hab
Aharah	uh-hair'uh
Aharhel	uh-hahr'hel
Ahasabi	uh-has'uh-b*i*
Ahasai	uh-hay's*i*

---

n not, ng sing, o hot, oh go, oi boy, oo foot, *oo* boot, oor poor, or for,
ou how, p pat, r run, s so, sh sure, t toe, th thin, *th* then, ts tsetse,
tw twin, uh ago, uhr her, v vow, w weather, y young, z zone, zh vision

Ahasbai	uh-haz'b*i*
Ahashtarite	uh-hash'tuh-r*i*t
Ahashuerus	uh-hash'y*oo*-er'uhs
Ahasuerus	uh-has'y*oo*-er'uhs
Ahava	uh-hay'vuh
Ahaz	ay'haz
Ahaziah	ay'huh-z*i*'uh
Ahban	ah'ban
Aher	ay'huhr
Ahi	ay'h*i*
Ahiah	uh-h*i*'uh
Ahiam	uh-h*i*'uhm
Ahian	uh-h*i*'uhn
Ahiezer	ay'h*i*-ee'zuhr
Ahihud	uh-h*i*'huhd
Ahijah	uh-h*i*'juh
Ahikam	uh-h*i*'kuhm
Ahikar	uh-h*i*'kahr
Ahilud	uh-h*i*'luhd
Ahimaaz	uh-him'ay-az
Ahiman	uh-h*i*'muhn
Ahimelech	uh-him'uh-lek
Ahimoth	uh-h*i*'moth
Ahinadab	uh-hin'uh-dab
Ahinoam	uh-hin'oh-uhm
Ahio	uh-h*i*'oh
Ahiqar	uh-h*i*'kahr
Ahira	uh-h*i*'ruh
Ahiram	uh-h*i*'ruhm
Ahiramite	uh-h*i*'ruh-m*i*t
Ahisamach	uh-his'uh-mak
Ahishahar	uh-hish'uh-hahr
Ahishar	uh-h*i*'shahr
Ahithophel	uh-hith'uh-fel
Ahitob	uh-h*i*'tob
Ahitub	uh-h*i*'tuhb
Ahlab	ah'lab
Ahlai	ah'l*i*
Ahoah	uh-hoh'uh
Ahoh	uh-hoh'
Ahohi	uh-hoh'h*i*
Ahohite	uh-hoh'h*i*t
Ahola	uh-hoh'luh
Aholah	uh-hoh'luh
Aholiab	uh-hoh'lee-ab

---

a cat, ah father, ahr lard, air care, aw jaw, ay pay, b bug, ch chew, d do,
e, eh pet, ee seem, er error, f fun, g good, h hot, hw whether, i it, *i* sky,
ihr ear, j joke, k king, kh ch as in German Buch, ks vex, kw quill, l love, m mat,

Aholibah	uh-hoh′li-buh
Aholibamah	uh-hoh′li-bah′mah
Ahumai	uh-hy*oo*′m*i*
Ahuzam	uh-h*oo*′zuhm
Ahuzzam	uh-huh′zuhm
Ahuzzath	uh-huh′zath
Ahzai	ah′z*i*
Ai	*i*, ay′*i*
Aiah	ay′yuh
Aiath	ay′yath
Aija	ay′juh
Aijalon	ay′juh-lon
Aijeleth	ay′juh-leth
Aijeleth-shahar	ay′juh-leth-shay′hahr
Aijeleth Shahar	ay′juh-leth-shay′hahr
Ain	ayn
ain	ah′yin
Airus	ay′ruhs
Ajah	ay′juh
Ajalon	aj′uh-lon
Akan	ay′kan
Akeldama	uh-kel′duh-muh
Akim	ay′kim
Akkad	ak′ad
Akkub	ak′uhb
Akrabattene	ak′ruh-bat′uh-nee
Akrabbim	uh-krab′im
Alameth	al′uh-muhth
Alammelech	uh-lam′uh-lek
Alamoth	al′uh-moth
Alcimus	al′si-muhs
Alema	al′uh-muh
Alemeth	al′uh-meth
aleph	ah′lef
Alexander	al′ig-zan′duhr
Alexandria	al′ig-zan′dree-uh
Alexandrian	al′ig-zan′dree-uhn
algum	al′guhm
Aliah	al′ee-uh
Alian	al′ee-uhn
Allammelech	uh-lam′uh-lek
alleluia	al′uh-*loo*′yuh
Allemeth	al′uh-meth
Allom	al′om
Allon	al′on

---

n not, ng sing, o hot, oh go, oi boy, oo foot, *oo* boot, oor poor, or for,
ou how, p pat, r run, s so, sh sure, t toe, th thin, *th* then, ts tsetse,
tw twin, uh ago, uhr her, v vow, w weather, y young, z zone, zh vision

Allon-bachuth	al'uhn-bak'uhth
Allon Bachuth	al'uhn-bak'uhth
Allonbacuth	al'uhn-bak'uhth
Allon-bacuth	al'uhn-bak'uhth
Allon Bacuth	al'uhn-bak'uhth
Allon Bakuth	al'uhn-bak'uhth
Almodad	al-moh'dad
Almon	al'muhn
Almondiblathaim	al'muhn-dib'luh-thay'im
Almon-diblathaim	al'muhn-dib'luh-thay'im
Almon Diblathaim	al'muhn-dib'luh-thay'im
almug	al'muhg
Alnathan	al-nay'thuhn
aloes	al'ohz
Aloth	ay'loth
alpha	al'fuh
Alphaeus	al-fee'uhs
Alpheus	al-fee'uhs
Altaneus	al'tuh-nee'uhs
Al-taschit	al-tas'kit
Al-taschith	al-tas'kith
Altashheth	al-tahsh'heth
Alush	ay'luhsh
Alvah	al'vuh
Alvan	al'vuhn
Amad	ay'mad
Amadatha	am'uh-day'thuh
Amal	ay'muhl
Amalek	am'uh-lek
Amalekite	uh-mal'uh-k*i*t
Amam	ay'mahm
Aman	ay'muhn
Amana	uh-may'nuh
Amariah	am'uh-r*i*'uh
Amarias	am'uh-r*i*'uhs
Amasa	uh-may'suh
Amasai	uh-may's*i*
Amashai	uh-mash'*i*
Amashsai	uh-mash's*i*
Amasi	uh-may's*i*
Amasiah	am'uh-s*i*'uh
Amatheis	am'uh-thee'uhs
Amathis	am'uh-this
Amaw	ay'maw
Amawite	ay'maw-*i*t

---

a cat, ah father, ahr lard, air care, aw jaw, ay pay, b bug, ch chew, d do,
e, eh pet, ee seem, er error, f fun, g good, h hot, hw whether, i it, *i* sky,
ihr ear, j joke, k king, kh ch as in German *Buch*, ks vex, kw quill, l love, m mat,

Amaziah	am'uh-zi'uh
amen	ah-men', ay'men'
Amen-em-ope	ah'men-em'oh-pi
Ami	ay'mi
Amiel	am'ee-uhl
Aminadab	uh-min'uh-dab
Amittai	uh-mit'i
Amizabad	uh-miz'uh-bad
Ammah	am'uh
Ammi	am'i
Ammidian	uh-mid'ee-uhn
Ammidoi	am'uh-doi
Ammiel	am'ee-uhl
Ammihud	uh-mi'huhd
Ammihur	uh-mi'huhr
Amminadab	uh-min'uh-dab
Amminadib	uh-min'uh-dib
Ammi-nadib	am'i-nay'dib
Ammishaddai	am-i-shad'i
Ammizabad	uh-miz'uh-bad
Ammon	am'uhn
Ammonite	am'uh-nit
Ammonitess	am'uh-nit-es
Amnon	am'non
Amok	ay'mok
Amon	am'uhn
Amorite	am'uh-rit
Amos	ay'muhs
Amoz	ay'muhz
Amphipolis	am-fip'uh-lis
Amplias	am'plee-uhs
Ampliatus	am'pli-ay'tuhs
Amram	am'ram
Amramite	am'ruh-mit
Amraphel	am'ruh-fel
Amri	am'ri
Amzi	am'zi
Anab	ay'nab
Anael	an'ay-uhl
Anah	ay'nuh
Anaharath	uh-nay'huh-rath
Anaiah	uh-nay'yuh
Anak	ay'nak
Anakim	an'uh-kim
Anakite	an'uh-kit

n not, ng sing, o hot, oh go, oi boy, oo foot, *oo* boot, oor poor, or for,
ou how, p pat, r run, s so, sh sure, t toe, th thin, *th* then, ts tsetse,
tw twin, uh ago, uhr her, v vow, w weather, y young, z zone, zh vision

Anam	ay'nuhm
Anamim	an'uh-mim
Anamite	an'uh-m*i*t
Anammelech	uh-nam'uh-lek
Anan	ay'nuhn
Anani	uh-nay'n*i*
Ananiah	an'uh-n*i*'uh
Ananias	an'uh-n*i*'uhs
Ananiel	uh-nan'ee-uhl
Anasib	an'uh-sib
Anath	ay'nath
anathema	uh-nath'uh-muh
Anathoth	an'uh-thoth
Anathothite	an'uh-thoh-th*i*t
Andrew	an'dr*oo*
Andronicus	an-dron'uh-kuhs
Anem	ay'nuhm
Aner	ay'nuhr
Anethothite	an'uh-thoh-th*i*t
Anetothite	an'uh-toh-th*i*t
Angle	an'guhl
Aniam	uh-n*i*'uhm
Anim	ay'nim
Anna	an'uh
Annaas	an'ay-uhs
Annan	an'uhn
Annas	an'uhs
Annias	uh-n*i*'uhs
Anniuth	uh-n*i*'uhth
Annunus	an'y*oo*-nuhs
Annuus	an'y*oo*-uhs
Anos	ay'nos
Anthothijah	an'thoh-th*i*'juh
Antichrist	an'tee-kr*i*st'
Antilebanon	an'tee-leb'uh-nuhn
Anti-lebanon	an'tee-leb'uh-nuhn
antimony	an'tuh-moh'nee
Antioch	an'tee-ok
Antiocha	an-t*i*'uh-kuh
Antiochian	an'tee-ok'ee-uhn
Antiochis	an-t*i*'uh-kis
Antiochus	an-t*i*'uh-kuhs
Antipas	an'tee-puhs
Antipater	an-tip'uh-tuhr
Antipatris	an-tip'uh-tris

---

a cat, ah father, ahr lard, air care, aw jaw, ay pay, b bug, ch chew, d do,
e, eh pet, ee seem, er error, f fun, g good, h hot, hw whether, i it, *i* sky,
ihr ear, j joke, k king, kh ch as in German *Buch*, ks vex, kw quill, l love, m mat,

Antothijah	an'toh-th*i*'juh
Antothite	an'tuh-th*i*t
Anub	ay'nuhb
Anus	ay'nuhs
Apame	uh-pay'mee
Apelles	uh-pel'eez
Aphairema	uh-fair'uh-muh
Apharsachite	uh-fahr'suh-k*i*t
Apharsathcite	uh-fahr'suth-k*i*t
Apharsite	uh-fahr's*i*t
Aphec	ay'fek
Aphek	ay'fek
Aphekah	uh-fee'kuh
Apherema	uh-fer'uh-muh
Apherra	uh-fer'uh
Aphiah	uh-f*i*'uh
Aphik	ay'fik
Aphrah	af'ruh
Aphses	af'seez
Apis	ay'pis
Apocalypse	uh-pok'uh-lips'
Apollonia	ap'uh-loh'nee-uh
Apollonius	ap'uh-loh'nee-uhs
Apollophanes	ap'uh-lof'uh-neez
Apollos	uh-pol'uhs
Apollyon	uh-pol'yuhn
apostasy	uh-pos'tuh-see
apostate	uh-pos'tayt'
apostle	uh-pos'uhl
apostleship	uh-pos'uhl-ship'
apostolic	ap'uh-stah'lik
Appaim	ap'ay-im
Apphia	af'ee-uh
Apphus	af'uhs
Appian	ap'ee-uhn
Appii Forum	ap'ee-*i*-for'uhm
Appius	ap'ee-uhs
Aqaba	ah'kuh-bah
Aqabah	ah'kuh-bah
Aquila	ak'wi-luh
Ar	ahr
Ara	air'uh
Arab	air'uhb
Arabah	air'uh-buh
Arabattine	air'uh-bat'uh-nee

---

n **not**, ng **sing**, o **hot**, oh **go**, oi **boy**, oo **foot**, *oo* **boot**, oor **poor**, or **for**,
ou **how**, p **pat**, r **run**, s **so**, sh **sure**, t **toe**, th **thin**, *th* **then**, ts **tsetse**,
tw **twin**, uh **ago**, uhr **her**, v **vow**, w **weather**, y **young**, z **zone**, zh **vision**

Arabia	uh-ray′bee-uh
Arabian	uh-ray′bee-uhn
Arabim	air′uh-bim
Arad	air′ad
Aradite	air′uh-d*i*t
Aradus	air′uh-duhs
Arah	air′uh
Aram	air′uhm
Aramaic	air′uh-may′ik
Aramean	air′uh-mee′uhn
Aramitess	air′uh-mi-tes
Arammaacah	air′uhm-may′uh-kuh
Aram-maacah	air′uhm-may′uh-kuh
Aram Maacah	air′uhm-may′uh-kuh
Aram-naharaim	air′uhm-nay-huh-ray′im
Aram Naharaim	air′uhm-nay-huh-ray′im
Aram-Zobah	air′uhm-zoh′buh
Aran	air′an
Ararat	air′uh-rat
Ararite	air′uh-r*i*t
Araunah	uh-raw′nuh
Arba	ahr′buh
Ar-baal	ahr-bay′uhl
Arbah	ahr′buh
Arbathite	ahr′buh-th*i*t
Arbatta	ahr-bat′uh
Arbattis	ahr-bat′is
Arbela	ahr-bee′luh
Arbite	ahr′b*i*t
Arbonai	ahr-boh′n*i*
archangel	ahrk′ayn-juhl
Archelaus	ahr′kuh-lay′uhs
Archevite	ahr′kuh-v*i*t
Archi	ahr′k*i*
Archippus	ahr-kip′uhs
Archite	ahr′k*i*t
Arcturus	ahrk-toor′uhs
Ard	ahrd
Ardat	ahr′dat
Ardath	ahr′dath
Ardite	ahr-d*i*t
Ardon	ahr′don
Areli	uh-ree′l*i*
Arelite	uh-ree′l*i*t
Areopagite	air′ee-op′uh-g*i*t

---

a cat, ah father, ahr lard, air care, aw jaw, ay pay, b bug, ch chew, d do,
e, eh pet, ee seem, er error, f fun, g good, h hot, hw whether, i it, *i* sky,
ihr ear, j joke, k king, kh ch as in German Buch, ks vex, kw quill, l love, m mat,

Areopagus	air′ee-op′uh-guhs
Ares	air′eez
Aretas	air′uh-tuhs
Areus	air′ee-uhs
Argob	ahr′gob
Ariarthes	air′ee-ahr′theez
Ariathes	air′ee-ay′theez
Aridai	air′uh-d*i*
Aridatha	air′uh-day′thuh
Arieh	air′ee-uh
Ariel	air′ee-uhl
Arimathaea	air′uh-muh-thee′uh
Arimathea	air′uh-muh-thee′uh
Arioch	air′ee-ok
Arisai	air′uh-s*i*
Aristarchus	air′is-tahr′kuhs
Aristobulus	air′is-tob′yuh-luhs
Arius	air′ee-uhs
Arkite	ahr′k*i*t
Armageddon	ahr′muh-ged′uhn
Armenia	ahr-mee′nee-uh
Armoni	ahr-moh′n*i*
Arna	ahr′nuh
Arnan	ahr′nuhn
Arni	ahr′n*i*
Arnon	ahr′nuhn
Arod	air′od
Arodi	air′uh-d*i*
Arodite	air′uh-d*i*t
Aroer	uh-roh′uhr
Aroerite	uh-roh′uh-r*i*t
Arom	air′uhm
Arpachshad	ahr-pak′shad
Arpad	ahr′pad
Arphad	ahr′fad
Arphaxad	ahr-fak′sad
Arsaces	ahr′suh-seez
Arsareth	ahr′suh-reth
Arsinoe	ahr-sin′oh-ee
Artaxerxes	ahr′tuh-zuhrk′seez
Artemas	ahr′tuh-muhs
Artemis	ahr′tuh-mis
Arubboth	uh-ruhb′oth
Aruboth	uh-r*oo*′both
Arumah	uh-r*oo*′mah

n not, ng sing, o hot, oh go, oi boy, oo foot, *oo* boot, oor poor, or for,
ou how, p pat, r run, s so, sh sure, t toe, th thin, *th* then, ts tsetse,
tw twin, uh ago, uhr her, v vow, w weather, y young, z zone, zh vision

Arvad	ahr'vad
Arvadite	ahr'vuh-d*i*t
Arza	ahr'zuh
Arzareth	ahr'zuh-reth
Asa	ay'suh
Asadias	as'uh-d*i*'uhs
Asael	as'ay-uhl
Asahel	as'uh-hel
Asahiah	as'uh-h*i*'uh
Asaiah	uh-zay'yuh
Asaias	uh-zay'yuhs
Asana	uh-sah'nuh
Asaph	ay'saf
Asaramel	uh-sair'uh-mel
Asareel	uh-sair'ee-uhl
Asarel	as'uh-rel
Asarelah	as'uh-ree'luh
Ascalon	as'kuh-lon
Aseas	as'ee-uhs
Asebebia	as'uh-bee'bee-uh
Asebia	uh-see'bee-uh
Asenath	as'uh-nath
Aser	ay'suhr
Aserer	ay'suh-ruhr
Ashan	ay'shuhn
Asharelah	ash'uh-ree'luh
Ashbea	ash'bee-uh
Ashbel	ash'bel
Ashbelite	ash'buh-l*i*t
Ashchenaz	ash'kuh-naz
Ashdod	ash'dod
Ashdodite	ash'duh-d*i*t
Ashdothite	ash'duh-th*i*t
Ashdoth-pisgah	ash'doth-piz'guh
Asher	ash'uhr
Asherah	uh-shihr'uh
Asherim	uh-shihr'im
Asherite	ash'uh-r*i*t
Asheroth	uh-shihr'oth
Ashhur	ash'uhr
Ashima	uh-sh*i*'muh
Ashimah	uh-sh*i*'muh
Ashkalon	ash'kuh-lon
Ashkelon	ash'kuh-lon
Ashkelonite	ash'kuh-luh-n*i*t

a cat, ah father, ahr lard, air care, aw jaw, ay pay, b bug, ch chew, d do,
e, eh pet, ee seem, er error, f fun, g good, h hot, hw whether, i it, *i* sky,
ihr ear, j joke, k king, kh ch as in German *Buch*, ks vex, kw quill, l love, m mat,

Ashkenaz	ash'kuh-naz
Ashnah	ash'nuh
Ashpenaz	ash'puh-naz
Ashriel	ash'ree-uhl
Ashtaroth	ash'tuh-roth
Ashterath	ash'tuh-rahth
Ashterathite	ash'tuh-ruh-th*i*t
Ashteroth	ash'tuh-roth
Ashterothkarnaim	ash'tuh-roth-kahr-nay'im
Ashteroth-karnaim	ash'tuh-roth-kahr-nay'im
Ashteroth Karnaim	ash'tuh-roth-kahr-nay'im
Ashtoreth	ash'tuh-reth
Ashur	ash'uhr
Ashurbanipal	ash'uhr-ban'uh-puhl
Ashuri	ash'uh-r*i*
Ashurite	ash'uh-r*i*t
Ashvath	ash'vath
Asia	ay'zhuh
Asian	ay'zhuhn
Asiarch	ay'zhee-ahrk
Asibias	as'uh-b*i*'uhs
Asidean	as'uh-dee'uhn
Asiel	as'ee-uhl
Asipha	uh-sif'uh
Askalon	as'kuh-lon
Askelon	as'kuh-lon
Asmodeus	az'moh-dee'uhs
Asnah	as'nuh
Asnapper	as-nap'uhr
Asom	ay'suhm
Aspalathus	as-pal'uh-thuhs
Aspatha	as-pay'thuh
Asphar	as'fahr
Aspharasus	as-fair'uh-suhs
Asriel	as'ree-uhl
Asrielite	as'ree-uh-l*i*t
Assabias	as'uh-b*i*'uhs
Assalimoth	uh-sal'uh-moth
Assanias	as'uh-n*i*'uhs
Assassin	uh-sas'uhn
Asser	as'uhr
Asshur	ash'uhr
Asshurim	ash'uh-rim
Asshurite	ash'uh-r*i*t
Assidean	as'uh-dee'uhn

---

n not, ng sing, o hot, oh go, oi boy, oo foot, *oo* boot, oor poor, or for,
ou how, p pat, r run, s so, sh sure, t toe, th thin, *th* then, ts tsetse,
tw twin, uh ago, uhr her, v vow, w weather, y young, z zone, zh vision

Assir	as'uhr
Assos	as'os
Assur	as'uhr
Assurbanipal	as'uhr-ban'uh-puhl
Assyria	uh-sihr'ee-uh
Assyrian	uh-sihr'ee-uhn
Astaroth	as'tuh-roth
Astarte	as-tahr'tee
Astath	as'tath
Astyages	as-ti'uh-jeez
Asuerus	azh'yoo-er'uhs
Asuppim	uh-suhp'im
Asur	ay'suhr
Aswan	as-wahn'
Asyncritus	uh-sin'kri-tuhs
Atad	ay'tad
Atarah	at'uh-ruh
Atargatis	uh-tahr'guh-tis
Ataroth	at'uh-roth'
Ataroth-adar	at'uh-roth-ad'uhr
Ataroth Adar	at'uh-roth-ad'uhr
Atarothaddar	at'uh-roth-ad'uhr
Ataroth-addar	at'uh-roth-ad'uhr
Ataroth Addar	at'uh-roth-ad'uhr
Atbash	at'bash
Ater	ay'tuhr
Aterezias	uh-ter'uh-zi'uhs
Athach	ay'thak
Athaiah	uh-thay'yuh
Athaliah	ath'uh-li'uh
Atharias	ath'uh-ri'uhs
Atharim	ath'uh-rim
Athbash	ath'bash
Athenian	uh-thee'nee-uhn
Athenobius	ath'uh-noh'bee-us
Athens	ath'inz
Athlai	ath'li
Atipha	uh-ti'fuh
Atroth	at'roth
Atrothbethjoab	at'roth-beth-joh'ab
Atroth-beth-joab	at'roth-beth-joh'ab
Atroth beth Joab	at'roth-beth-joh'ab
Atrothshophan	at'roth-shoh'fan
Atroth-shophan	at'roth-shoh'fan
Atroth Shophan	at'roth-shoh'fan

a cat, ah father, ahr lard, air care, aw jaw, ay pay, b bug, ch chew, d do,
e, eh pet, ee seem, er error, f fun, g good, h hot, hw whether, i it, i sky,
ihr ear, j joke, k king, kh ch as in German Buch, ks vex, kw quill, l love, m mat,

Attai	at'*i*
Attalia	at'uh-li'uh
Attalus	at'uh-luhs
Attharates	ath'uh-ray'teez
Attharias	ath'uh-ri'uhs
Augia	aw'jee-uh
Augusta	aw-guhs'tuh
Augustan	aw-guhs'tuhn
Augustus	aw-guhs'tuhs
Auranus	aw-ray'nuhs
Auteas	aw-tee'uhs
Ava	ay'vuh
Avaran	av'uh-ran
Aven	ay'ven
Avim	ay'vim
Avite	ay'vi*t*
Avith	ay'vith
Avva	av'uh
Avvim	av'im
Avvite	av'*i*t
ayin	i'yin
Ayyah	ah'yuh
Azael	ay'zay-uhl
Azaelus	az'uh-ee'luhs
Azal	ay'zuhl
Azaliah	az'uh-li'uh
Azaniah	az'uh-ni'uh
Azaphion	uh-zay'fee-uhn
Azara	az'uh-ruh
Azarael	az'uh-ray'uhl
Azareel	az'uh-ree'uhl
Azarel	az'uh-rel
Azariah	az'uh-ri'uh
Azariahu	az'uh-ri'uh-hy*oo*
Azarias	az'uh-ri'uhs
Azaru	az'uh-r*oo*
Azaryahu	az'uhr-yah'h*oo*
Azaz	ay'zaz
Azazel	uh-zay'zuhl
Azaziah	az'uh-zi'uh
Azbazareth	az-baz'uh-reth
Azbuk	az'buhk
Azekah	uh-zee'kuh
Azel	ay'zuhl
Azem	ay'zuhm

n not, ng sing, o hot, oh go, oi boy, oo foot, *oo* boot, oor poor, or for,
ou how, p pat, r run, s so, sh sure, t toe, th thin, *th* then, ts tsetse,
tw twin, uh ago, uhr her, v vow, w weather, y young, z zone, zh vision

Azephurith	uh-zef′uh-rith
Azetas	uh-zee′tuhs
Azgad	az′gad
Azia	az″ee-uh
Aziei	az′uh-ee′*i*
Aziel	ay′zee-uhl
Aziza	uh-z*i*′′zuh
Azmaveth	az′muh-veth
Azmon	az′mon
Aznothtabor	az′noth-tay′buhr
Aznoth-tabor	az′noth-tay′buhr
Aznoth Tabor	az′noth-tay′buhr
Azor	ay′zor
Azotus	uh-zoh′tuhs
Azriel	az′ree-uhl
Azrikam	az′ri-kuhm
Azubah	uh-zoo′buh
Azur	ay′zuhr
Azuran	uh-zoo′ruhn
Azzah	az′uh
Azzan	az′uhn
Azzur	az′uhr

B

Baal	bay′uhl, bah-ahl′
Baala	bay′uh-luh, bah′uh-luh
Baalah	bay′uh-luh, bah′uh-luh
Baalath	bay′uh-lath, bah′uh-lath
Baalathbeer	bay′uh-lath-bee′uhr, bah′uh-lath-bee′uhr
Baalath-beer	bay′uh-lath-bee′uhr, bay′uh-lath-bee′uhr
Baalath Beer	bay′uh-lath-bee′uhr, bah′uh-lath-bee′uhr
Baalberith	bay′uhl-bi-rith′, bah′uhl-bi-rith′
Baal-berith	bay′uhl-bi-rith′, bah′uhl-bi-rith′
Baale	bay′uh-lee, bah′uh-lee
Baalejudah	bay′uh-lee-joo′duh, bah′uh-lee-joo′duh
Baale-judah	bay′uh-lee-joo′duh, bah′uh-lee-joo′duh
Baale Judah	bay′uh-lee-joo′duh, bah-uh-lee-joo′duh
Baalgad	bay′uhl-gad′, bah′uhl-gad′
Baal-gad	bay′uhl-gad′, bah′uhl-gad′
Baal Gad	bay′uhl-gad′, bah′uhl-gad′

a cat, ah father, ahr lard, air care, aw jaw, ay pay, b bug, ch chew, d do,
e, eh pet, ee seem, er error, f fun, g good, h hot, hw whether, i it, *i* sky,
ihr ear, j joke, k king, kh ch as in German *Buch*, ks vex, kw quill, l love, m mat,

Baalhamon	bay'uhl-hay'muhn, bah'uhl-hay'muhn
Baal-hamon	bay'uhl-hay'muhn, bah'uhl-hay'muhn
Baal Hamon	bay'uhl-hay'muhn, bah'uhl-hay'muhn
Baalhanan	bay'uhl-hay'nuhn, bah'uhl-hay'nuhn
Baal-hanan	bay'uhl-hay'nuhn, bah'uhl-hay'nuhn
Baal Hanan	bay'uhl-hay'nuhn, bah'uhl-hay'nuhn
Baalhazor	bay'uhl-hay'zor, bah'uhl-hay'zor
Baal-hazor	bay'uhl-hay'zor, bah'uhl-hay'zor
Baal Hazor	bay'uhl-hay'zor, bah'uhl-hay'zor
Baalhermon	bay'uhl-huhr'muhn, bah'uhl-huhr'muhn
Baal-hermon	bay'uhl-huhr'muhn, bah'uhl-huhr'muhn
Baal Hermon	bay'uhl-huhr'muhn, bah'uhl-huhr'muhn
Baali	bay'uh-li, bah'uh-li
Baaliada	bay'uh-li'uh-duh, bah'uh-li'uh-duh
Baalim	bay'uh-lim, bah'uh-lim
Baalis	bay'uh-lis, bah'uh-lis
Baalmeon	bay'uhl-mee'on, bah'uhl-mee'on
Baal-meon	bay'uhl-mee'on, bah'uhl-mee'on
Baal Meon	bay'uhl-mee'on, bah'uhl-mee'on
Baalpeor	bay'uhl-pee'or, bah'uhl-pee'or
Baal-peor	bay'uhl-pee'or, bah'uhl-pee'or
Baal Peor	bay'uhl-pee'or, bah'uhl-pee'or
Baalperazim	bay'uhl-pi-ray'zim, bah'uhl-pi-ray'zim
Baal-perazim	bay'uhl-pi-ray'zim, bah'uhl-pi-ray'zim
Baal Perazim	bay'uhl-pi-ray'zim, bah'uhl-pi-ray'zim
Baalsamus	bay'uhl-say'muhs, bah'uhl-say'muhs
Baal-shalisha	bay'uhl-shal'uh-shuh, bah'uhl-shal'uh'shuh
Baal Shalisha	bay'uhl-shal'uh-shuh, bah'uhl-shal'uh'shuh
Baalshalishah	bay'uhl-shal'uh-shuh, bah'uhl-shal'uh'shuh
Baal-shalishah	bay'uhl-shal'uh-shuh, bah'uhl-shal'uh-shuh
Baal Shalishah	bay'uhl-shal'uh-shuh, bah'uhl-shal'uh-shuh
Baaltamar	bay'uhl-tay'mahr, bah'uhl-tay'mahr
Baal-tamar	bay'uhl-tay'mahr, bah'uhl-tay'muhr
Baal Tamar	bay'uhl-tay'mahr, bah'uhl-tay'muhr
Baalzebub	bay'uhl-zee'buhb, bah'uhl-zee'buhb
Baal-zebub	bay'uhl-zee'buhb, bah'uhl-zee'buhb
Baalzephon	bay'uhl-zee'fon, bah'uhl-zee'fon
Baal-zephon	bay'uhl-zee'fon, bah'uhl-zee'fon
Baal Zephon	bay'uhl-zee'fon, bah'uhl-zee'fon
Baana	bay'uh-nuh
Baanah	bay'uh-nuh
Baanias	bay'uh-ni'uhs
Baara	bay'uh-ruh
Baaseiah	bay'uh-see'yuh
Baasha	bay'uh-shuh

n not, ng sing, o hot, oh go, oi boy, oo foot, *oo* boot, oor poor, or for,
ou how, p pat, r run, s so, sh sure, t toe, th thin, *th* then, ts tsetse,
tw twin, uh ago, uhr her, v vow, w weather, y young, z zone, zh vision

Babel	bay'buhl
Babi	bay'b*i*
Babylon	bab'uh-luhn
Babylonia	bab'uh-loh'nee-uh
Babylonian	bab'uh-loh'nee-uhn
Babylonish	bab'uh-loh'nish
Baca	bay'kuh
Bacchides	bak'uh-deez
Bacchurus	ba-kyoor'uhs
Bacenor	buh-see'nor
Bachrite	bak'r*i*t
Bachuth	bay'kuhth
Bacuth	bay'kuhth
Baean	bee'uhn
Bagathan	bag'uh-than
Bago	bay'goh
Bagoas	buh-goh'uhs
Bagoi	bay'goi
Bah	bah
Baharum	buh-hair'uhm
Baharumite	buh-hair'uh-m*i*t
Bahurim	buh-hyoor'im
Baiterus	b*i*'tuh-ruhs
Baither	b*i*'thuhr
Bajith	bay'jith
Bakbakkar	bak-bak'uhr
Bakbuk	bak'buhk
Bakbukiah	bak'buh-k*i*'uh
Bakuth	bay'kuhth
Balaam	bay'luhm
Balac	bay'lak
Baladan	bal'uh-duhn
Balah	bay'luh
Balak	bay'lak
Balamo	bay'luh-moh
Balamon	bal'uh-muhn
Balasamus	buh-las'uh-muhs
Balbaim	bal-bay'im
Baldad	bal'dad
Balnuus	bal'noo-uhs
Balthasar	bal-thaz'uhr
Bamah	bay'muh
Bamoth	bay'moth
Bamothbaal	bay'moth-bay'uhl
Bamoth-baal	bay'moth-bay'uhl

a cat, ah father, ahr lard, air care, aw jaw, ay pay, b bug, ch chew, d do,
e, eh pet, ee seem, er error, f fun, g good, h hot, hw whether, i it, *i* sky,
ihr ear, j joke, k king, kh ch as in German *Buch*, ks vex, kw quill, l love, m mat,

22

Bamoth Baal	bay'moth-bay'uhl
Ban	ban
Banaias	buh-nay'yuhs
Bani	bay'n*i*
Bannaia	buh-nay'yuh
Bannas	ban'uhs
Bannus	ban'uhs
Banuas	ban'yoo-uhs
Baptist	bap'tist
Baptizer	bap't*i*-zuhr
Barabbas	buh-rab'uhs
Barachel	bair'uh-kuhl
Barachiah	bair'uh-k*i*'uh
Barachias	bair'uh-k*i*'uhs
Barah	bair'uh
Barak	bair'ak
Barakel	bair'uh-kuhl
barbarian	bahr-bair'ee-uhn
Barhumite	bahr-hy*oo*'m*i*t
Bariah	buh-r*i*'uh
Bar-jesus	bahr-jee'zuhs
Barjona	bahr-joh'nuh
Bar-jona	bahr-joh'nuh
Bar-jonah	bahr-joh'nuh
Barkos	bahr'kos
Barnabas	bahr'nuh-buhs
Barnea	bahr'nee-uh
Barodis	buh-roh'dis
Barsabas	bahr'suh-buhs
Barsabbas	bahr-sab'uhs
Bartacus	bahr'tuh-kuhs
Bartholomew	bahr-thol'uh-my*oo*
Bartimaeus	bahr'tuh-mee'uhs
Bartimeus	bahr'tuh-mee'uhs
Baruch	bair'uhk
Barzillai	bahr-zil'*i*
Basaloth	bas'uh-loth
Bascama	bas'kuh-muh
Basemath	bas'uh-math
Bashan	bay'shuhn
Bashan-havoth-jair	bay'shuhn-hay'voth-jay'uhr
Bashemath	bash'uh-math
Baskama	bas'kuh-muh
Basmath	bas'math
Bastai	bas't*i*

n **not**, ng **sing**, o **hot**, oh **go**, oi **boy**, oo **foot**, *oo* **boot**, oor **poor**, or **for**,
ou **how**, p **pat**, r **run**, s **so**, sh **sure**, t **toe**, th **thin**, *th* **then**, ts **tsetse**,
tw **twin**, uh **ago**, uhr **her**, v **vow**, w **weather**, y **young**, z **zone**, zh **vision**

Bat-gader	bat-gay′duhr
Bath	bath
bath	bath
Bathrabbim	bath-rab′im
Bath-rabbim	bath-rab′im
Bath Rabbim	bath-rab′im
Bathsheba	bath-shee′buh
Bath-sheba	bath-shee′buh
Bathshua	bath-sh*oo*′uh
Bath-shua	bath-sh*oo*′uh
Bathzacharias	bath′zak-uh-r*i*′uhs
Bavai	bay′v*i*
Bavvai	bav′*i*
Baz	baz
Bazlith	baz′lith
Bazluth	baz′luhth
Bealiah	bee′uh-l*i*′uh
Bealoth	bee′uh-loth
Bebai	bee′b*i*
Becher	bee′kuhr
Becherite	bee′kuh-r*i*t
Bechorath	bi-kor′ath
Bechrite	bek′r*i*t
Becorath	bi-kor′ath
Bectileth	bek′tuh-leth
Bedad	bee′dad
Bedan	bee′dan
Bedeiah	bi-dee′yah
Beeliada	bee′uh-l*i*′uh-duh
Beelsarus	bee-el′suh-ruhs
Beeltethmus	bee′uhl-teth′muhs
Beelzebub	bee-el′zi-buhb
Beelzebul	bee-el′zi-buhl
Beer	bee′uhr
Beera	bee′uh-ruh
Beerah	bee′uh-ruh
Beerelim	bee′uhr-ee′lim
Beer-elim	bee′uhr-ee′lim
Beer Elim	bee′uhr-ee′lim
Beeri	bee′uhr-*i*
Beerlahairoi	bee′uhr-luh-h*i*′roi
Beer-lahai-roi	bee′uhr-luh-h*i*′roi
Beer Lahai Roi	bee′uhr-luh-h*i*′roi
Beeroth	bee′uh-roth
Beeroth Bene-Jaakan	bee′uh-roth-ben′i-jay′uh-kuhn

---

a cat, ah father, ahr lard, air care, aw jaw, ay pay, b bug, ch chew, d do,
e, eh pet, ee seem, er error, f fun, g good, h hot, hw whether, i it, *i* sky,
ihr ear, j joke, k king, kh ch as in German *Buch*, ks vex, kw quill, l love, m mat,

Beerothite	bee'uh-ruh-th*i*t
Beersheba	bee'uhr-shee'buh
Beer-sheba	bee'uhr-shee'buh
Beeshterah	bee-esh'tuh-ruh
Be-eshterah	bee-esh'tuh-ruh
Be Eshterah	bee-esh'tuh-ruh
Beesh-terah	bee-esh'tuh-ruh
Behemoth	bi-hee'muhth
beka	bee'kuh
bekah	bee'kuh
Beker	bee'kuhr
Bekerite	bee'kuh-r*i*t
Bel	bel
Bela	bee'luh
Belah	bee'luh
Belaite	bee'lay-*i*t
Belemus	bel'uh-muhs
Belial	bee'lee-uhl
Belmaim	bel-may'im
Belmain	bel'mayn
Belmen	bel'muhn
Belnuus	bel'n*oo*-uhs
Belshazzar	bel-shaz'uhr
Belteshazzar	bel'ti-shaz'uhr
Beltethmus	bel-teth'muhs
Bemidbar	buh-mid'bahr
Ben	ben
Benabinadab	ben'uh-bin'uh-dab
Ben-abinadab	ben'uh-bin'uh-dab
Benaiah	bi-nay'yuh
Benammi	ben-am'*i*
Ben-ammi	ben-am'*i*
Bendeker	ben-dee'kuhr
Ben-deker	ben-dee'kuhr
Bene	ben'ee
Beneberak	ben'ee-bihr'ak
Bene-berak	ben'ee-bihr'ak
Bene Berak	ben'ee-bihr'ak
Benejaakan	ben'ee-jay'uh-kuhn
Bene-jaakan	ben'ee-jay'uh-kuhn
Bene Jaakan	ben'ee-jay'uh-kuhn
Bengeber	ben-gee'buhr
Ben-geber	ben-gee'buhr
Bengui	ben'gy*oo*-*i*
Benhadad	ben-hay'dad

n **n**ot, ng si**ng**, o h**o**t, oh g**o**, oi b**oy**, oo f**oo**t, *oo* b**oo**t, oor p**oor**, or f**or**, ou h**ow**, p **p**at, r **r**un, s **s**o, sh **s**ure, t **t**oe, th **th**in, *th* **th**en, ts **ts**etse, tw **tw**in, uh **a**go, uhr h**er**, v **v**ow, w **w**eather, y **y**oung, z **z**one, zh vi**s**ion

Ben-hadad	ben-hay′dad
Benhail	ben-hay′uhl
Ben-hail	ben-hay′uhl
Benhanan	ben-hay′nuhn
Ben-hanan	ben-hay′nuhn
Benhesed	ben-hee′sed
Ben-hesed	ben-hee′sed
Ben-hinnom	ben-hin′uhm
Ben Hinnom	ben-hin′uhm
Benhur	ben-huhr′
Ben-hur	ben-huhr′
Beninu	bi-ni′nyoo
Ben-jahaziel	ben′juh-hay′zee-uhl
Benjamin	ben′juh-muhn
Benjaminite	ben′juh-muh-nit
Benjamite	ben′juh-mit
Ben-josiphiah	ben′jos-uh-fi′uh
Beno	bee′noh
Benob	bee′nob
Benoni	ben-oh′ni
Ben-oni	ben-oh′ni
Benoth	bee′noth
Benzoheth	ben-zoh′heth
Ben-zoheth	ben-zoh′heth
Beon	bee′on
Beor	bee′or
Bera	bihr′uh
Beracah	ber′uh-kuh
Berachah	ber′uh-kuh
Berachiah	ber′uh-ki′uh
Beraiah	bi-ray′yuh
Berakiah	ber′uh-ki′uh
Berea	bi-ree′uh
Berean	bi-ree′uhn
Berechiah	ber′uh-ki′uh
Bered	bihr′ed
Berekiah	ber′uh-ki′uh
Berenice	buhr-uh-nees′
Bereshith	ber′uh-shith
Beri	bihr′i
Beriah	bi-ri′uh
Beriite	bi-ri′it
Berite	bihr′it
Berith	bi-rith′
Bernice	buhr-nees′

---

a cat, ah father, ahr lard, air care, aw jaw, ay pay, b bug, ch chew, d do,
e, eh pet, ee seem, er error, f fun, g good, h hot, hw whether, i it, *i* sky,
ihr ear, j joke, k king, kh ch as in German *Buch*, ks vex, kw quill, l love, m mat,

Berodach-baladan	buh-roh′dak-bal′uh-duhn
Beroea	bi-ree′uh
Beroean	bi-ree′uhn
Beroth	bihr′oth
Berothah	bi-roh′thuh
Berothai	bi-roh′th*i*
Berothite	bihr′uh-th*i*t
Berzelus	buhr-zee′luhs
Besai	bee′s*i*
Bescaspasmys	bes′kuhs-paz′muhs
Beseth	bee′seth
Besodeiah	bes′uh-dee′yah
besom	bee′suhm
Besor	bee′sor
Betah	bee′tuh
Betane	bet′uh-nee
Beten	bee′tuhn
beth	beth
Bethabara	beth-ab′uh-ruh
Beth Acacia	beth′uh-kay′shuh
Beth-achzib	beth-ak′zib
Bethanath	beth-ay′nath
Beth-anath	beth-ay′nath
Beth Anath	beth-ay′nath
Bethanoth	beth-ay′noth
Beth-anoth	beth-ay′noth
Beth Anoth	beth-ay′noth
Bethany	beth′uh-nee
Beth Aphrah	beth-af′ruh
Betharabah	beth-air′uh-buh
Beth-arabah	beth-air′uh-buh
Beth Arabah	beth-air′uh-buh
Beth-aram	beth-air′uhm
Betharbel	beth-ahr′buhl
Beth-arbel	beth-ahr′buhl
Beth Arbel	beth-ahr′buhl
Bethashbea	beth-ash′bee-uh
Beth-ashbea	beth-ash′bee-uh
Beth Ashbea	beth-ash′bee-uh
Bethasmoth	beth-as′moth
Beth-asmoth	beth-as′moth
Beth-astharoth	beth-as′thuh-roth
Bethaven	beth-ay′vuhn
Beth-aven	beth-ay′vuhn
Beth Aven	beth-ay′vuhn

n not, ng sing, o hot, oh go, oi boy, oo foot, *oo* boot, oor poor, or for,
ou how, p pat, r run, s so, sh sure, t toe, th thin, *th* then, ts tsetse,
tw twin, uh ago, uhr her, v vow, w weather, y young, z zone, zh vision

Bethazmaveth	beth-az'muh-veth
Beth-azmaveth	beth-az'muh-veth
Beth Azmaveth	beth-az'muh-veth
Bethbaalmeon	beth-bay'uhl-mee'on
Beth-baal-meon	beth-bay'uhl-mee'on
Beth Baal Meon	beth-bay'uhl-mee'on
Bethbarah	beth-bair'uh
Beth-barah	beth-bair'uh
Beth Barah	beth-bair'uh
Bethbasi	beth-bay's*i*
Beth-basi	beth-bay's*i*
Beth-birei	beth-bihr'ee-*i*
Bethbiri	beth-bihr'*i*
Beth-biri	beth-bihr'*i*
Beth Biri	beth-bihr'*i*
Bethcar	beth-kahr'
Beth-car	beth-kahr'
Beth Car	beth-kahr'
Bethdagon	beth-day'gon
Beth-dagon	beth-day'gon
Beth Dagon	beth-day'gon
Bethdiblathaim	beth'dib-luh-thay'im
Beth-diblathaim	beth'dib-luh-thay'im
Beth Diblathaim	beth'dib-luh-thay'im
Betheden	beth-ee'duhn
Beth-eden	beth-ee'duhn
Beth Eden	beth-ee'duhn
Betheglaim	beth-eg'lay-im
Beth-eglaim	beth-eg'lay-im
Beth Eglaim	beth-eg'lay-im
Betheked	beth-ee'kid
Beth-eked	beth-ee'kid
Beth Eked	beth-ee'kid
Beth-eked-haroim	beth-ee'kid-hah-roh'im
Bethel	beth'uhl
Beth-el	beth'uhl
Bethelite	beth'uh-l*i*t
Beth-elite	beth'uh-l*i*t
Bethelsarezer	beth'uhl-suh-ree'zuhr
Bethemek	beth-ee'mik
Beth-emek	beth-ee'mik
Beth Emek	beth-ee'mik
Bether	bee'thuhr
Bethesda	buh-thez'duh
Bethezel	beth-ee'zuhl

---

a cat, ah father, ahr lard, air care, aw jaw, ay pay, b bug, ch chew, d do,
e, eh pet, ee seem, er error, f fun, g good, h hot, hw whether, i it, *i* sky,
ihr ear, j joke, k king, kh ch as in German Buch, ks vex, kw quill, l love, m mat,

Beth-ezel	beth-ee′zuhl
Beth Ezel	beth-ee′zuhl
Bethgader	beth-gay′duhr
Beth-gader	beth-gay′duhr
Beth Gader	beth-gay′duhr
Bethgamul	beth-gay′muhl
Beth-gamul	beth-gay′muhl
Beth Gamul	beth-gay′muhl
Bethgilgal	beth-gil′gal
Beth-gilgal	beth-gil′gal
Beth Gilgal	beth-gil′gal
Beth-haccerem	beth-hak′uh-rem
Beth Haccerem	beth-hak′uh-rem
Bethhaccherem	beth-hak′uh-rem
Beth-haccherem	beth-hak′uh-rem
Beth Haccherem	beth-hak′uh-rem
Bethhaggan	beth-hag′uhn
Beth-haggan	beth-hag′uhn
Beth Haggan	beth-hag′uhn
Beth Hakkerem	beth′hak′uh-rem
Beth-hanan	beth-hay′nuhn
Bethharam	beth-hair′uhm
Beth-haram	beth-hair′uhm
Beth Haram	beth-hair′uhm
Bethharan	beth-hair′uhn
Beth-haran	beth-hair′uhn
Beth Haran	beth-hair′uhn
Beth-hogla	beth-hog′luh
Bethhoglah	beth-hog′luh
Beth-hoglah	beth-hog′luh
Beth Hoglah	beth-hog′luh
Bethhoron	beth-hor′uhn
Beth-horon	beth-hor′uhn
Beth Horon	beth-hor′uhn
Bethjeshimoth	beth-jesh′uh-moth
Beth-jeshimoth	beth-jesh′uh-moth
Beth Jeshimoth	beth-jesh′uh-moth
Beth-jesimoth	beth-jes′uh-moth
Beth Jesimoth	beth-jes′uh-moth
Bethleaphrah	beth′li-af′ruh
Beth-le-aphrah	beth′li-af′ruh
Beth-leaphrah	beth′li-af′ruh
Bethlebaoth	beth′li-bay′oth
Beth-lebaoth	beth′li-bay′oth
Beth Lebaoth	beth′li-bay′oth

n not, ng sing, o hot, oh go, oi boy, oo foot, *oo* boot, oor poor, or for,
ou how, p pat, r run, s so, sh sure, t toe, th thin, *th* then, ts tsetse,
tw twin, uh ago, uhr her, v vow, w weather, y young, z zone, zh vision

Bethlehem	beth′li-hem
Beth-lehem	beth′li-hem
Bethlehem Ephratah	beth′li-hem-ef′ruh-tuh
Bethlehem-ephrathah	beth′li-hem-ef′ruh-thuh
Bethlehemite	beth′li-heh-m*i*t
Beth-lehemite	beth′li-heh-m*i*t
Beth-lehem-judah	beth′li-hem-j*oo*′duh
Beth-lomon	beth-loh′muhn
Bethmaacah	beth-may′uh-kuh
Beth-maacah	beth-may′uh-kuh
Beth-maachah	beth-may′uh-kuh
Beth Maachah	beth-may′uh-kuh
Bethmarcaboth	beth-mahr′kuh-both
Beth-marcaboth	beth-mahr′kuh-both
Beth Marcaboth	beth-mahr′kuh-both
Bethmeon	beth-mee′on
Beth-meon	beth-mee′on
Beth Meon	beth-mee′on
Bethmillo	beth-mil′oh
Beth-millo	beth-mil′oh
Beth Millo	beth-mil′oh
Bethnimrah	beth-nim′ruh
Beth-nimrah	beth-nim′ruh
Beth Nimrah	beth-nim′ruh
Beth-ophrah	beth-of′ruh
Beth Ophrah	beth-of′ruh
Beth-oron	beth-or′uhn
Beth-palet	beth-pay′let
Bethpazzez	beth-paz′iz
Beth-pazzez	beth-paz′iz
Beth Pazzez	beth-paz′iz
Bethpelet	beth-pee′lit
Beth-pelet	beth-pee′lit
Beth Pelet	beth-pee′lit
Bethpeor	beth-pee′or
Beth-peor	beth-pee′or
Beth Peor	beth-pee′or
Bethphage	beth′fuh-jee
Beth-phelet	beth-fee′lit
Bethrapha	beth-ray′fuh
Beth-rapha	beth-ray′fuh
Beth Rapha	beth-ray′fuh
Bethrehob	beth-ree′hob
Beth-rehob	beth-ree′hob
Beth Rehob	beth-ree′hob

---

a cat, ah father, ahr lard, air care, aw jaw, ay pay, b bug, ch chew, d do,
e, eh pet, ee seem, er error, f fun, g good, h hot, hw whether, i it, *i* sky,
ihr ear, j joke, k king, kh ch as in German *Buch*, ks vex, kw quill, l love, m mat,

Bethsabee	beth-say'buh-ee
Bethsaida	beth-say'uh-duh
Beth-saida	beth-say'uh-duh
Bethsamos	beth-sam'os
Bethsan	beth-san'
Bethshan	beth-shan'
Beth-shan	beth-shan'
Beth Shan	beth-shan'
Bethshean	beth-shee'uhn
Beth-shean	beth-shee'uhn
Beth Shean	beth-shee'uhn
Bethshemesh	beth-sheh'mish
Beth-shemesh	beth-sheh'mish
Beth Shemesh	beth-sheh'mish
Bethshemite	beth-shem'*i*t
Beth-shemite	beth-shem'*i*t
Bethshittah	beth-shit'uh
Beth-shittah	beth-shit'uh
Beth Shittah	beth-shit'uh
Bethsura	beth-soor'uh
Bethtappuah	beth-tap'yoo-uh
Beth-tappuah	beth-tap'yoo-uh
Beth Tappuah	beth-tap'yoo-uh
Bethtogarmah	beth'toh-gahr'muh
Beth-togarmah	beth'toh-gahr'muh
Beth Togarmah	beth'toh-gahr'muh
Bethuel	bi-thy*oo*'uhl
Bethul	beth'uhl
Bethulia	bi-th*oo*'lee-uh
Beth-zaith	beth-zay'ith
Bethzatha	beth-zay'thuh
Beth-zatha	beth-zay'thuh
Beth-zechariah	beth-zek'uh-r*i*'uh
Bethzur	beth-zuhr'
Beth-zur	beth-zuhr'
Beth Zur	beth-zuhr'
Betolius	bi-toh'lee-uhs
Betomasthaim	bet'uh-mas-thay'im
Betomastham	bet'uh-mas'thuhm
Betomesthaim	bet'uh-mis-thay'im
Betomestham	bet'uh-mes'thuhm
Betonim	bet'uh-nim
Beulah	by*oo*'luh
Bezaanannim	bi-zay'uh-nan'im
Bezai	bee'z*i*

n not, ng sing, o hot, oh go, oi boy, oo foot, *oo* boot, oor poor, or for,
ou how, p pat, r run, s so, sh sure, t toe, th thin, *th* then, ts tsetse,
tw twin, uh ago, uhr her, v vow, w weather, y young, z zone, zh vision

Bezaleel	bi-zal'ee-uhl
Bezalel	bez'uh-lel
Bezek	bee'zik
Bezer	bee'zuhr
Bezeth	bee'zith
Bezetha	bee'zuh-thuh
Biatas	bi'uh-tuhs
Bichri	bik'ri
Bichrite	bik'rit
Bicri	bik'ri
Bidkar	bid'kahr
Bigtha	big'thuh
Bigthan	big'thuhn
Bigthana	big'thuh-nuh
Bigvai	big'vi
Bikri	bik'ri
Bildad	bil'dad
Bileam	bil'ee-uhm
Bilgah	bil'guh
Bilgai	bil'gi
Bilhah	bil'huh
Bilhan	bil'han
Bilshan	bil'shan
Bimhal	bim'hal
Binea	bin'ee-uh
Binnui	bin'yoo-i
Birei	bihr'ee-i
Biri	bihr'i
Birsha	bihr'shuh
Birzaith	bihr-zay'ith
Birzavith	bihr-zay'vith
Bishlam	bish'luhm
bishop	bish'uhp
Bithia	bith'ee-uh
Bithiah	bi-thi'uh
Bithron	bith'ron
Bithynia	bi-thin'ee-uh
Biziothiah	biz'ee-oh-thi'uh
Bizjothjah	biz-joth'juh
Biztha	biz'thuh
Blastus	blas'tuhs
Boanerges	boh'uh-nuhr'jeez
Boaz	boh'az
Boccas	bok'uhs
Bocheru	boh'kuh-roo

---

a cat, ah father, ahr lard, air care, aw jaw, ay pay, b bug, ch chew, d do,
e, eh pet, ee seem, er error, f fun, g good, h hot, hw whether, i it, *i* sky,
ihr ear, j joke, k king, kh ch as in German *Buch*, ks vex, kw quill, l love, m mat,

Bochim	boh'kim
Bohan	boh'han
Bokeru	boh'kuh-r*oo*
Bokim	boh'kim
Booths	b*oo*ths
Booz	boh'oz
Borashan	bor-ay'shuhn
Bor-ashan	bor-ay'shuhn
Bor Ashan	bor-ay'shuhn
Borith	bor'ith
Boscath	bos'kath
Bosketh	bos'kith
Bosor	boh'sor
Bosora	bos'uh-ruh
Bougaean	b*oo*-gee'uhn
Bozez	boh'ziz
Bozkath	boz'kath
Boznai	boz'n*i*
Bozrah	boz'ruh
Bubastis	by*oo*-bas'tis
Bukki	buhk'*i*
Bukkiah	buh-k*i*'uh
Bul	bool
Bunah	by*oo*'nuh
Bunni	buhn'*i*
Buz	buhz
Buzi	by*oo*'z*i*
Buzite	by*oo*'z*i*t
Byblos	bib'los

C

Caanan	kay'uh-nuhn
cab	kab
Cabbon	kab'uhn
Cabul	kay'buhl
Caddis	kad'is
Cades	kay'deez
Cades-barne	kay'dees-bahr'nee
Cadmiel	kad'mee-uhl
Caesar	see'zuhr

n **n**ot, ng si**ng**, o h**o**t, oh g**o**, oi b**oy**, oo f**oo**t, *oo* b**oo**t, oor p**oor**, or f**or**,
ou h**ow**, p **p**at, r **r**un, s **s**o, sh **s**ure, t **t**oe, th **th**in, *th* **th**en, ts **ts**etse,
tw **tw**in, uh **a**go, uhr h**er**, v **v**ow, w **w**eather, y **y**oung, z **z**one, zh vi**s**ion

Caesaraea	ses'uh-ree'uh
Caesaraea-Philippi	ses'uh-ree'uh-fil-ip'*i*, ses'uh-ree'uh-fil'i-p*i*
Caesarea	ses'uh-ree'uh
Caesarea Philippi	ses'uh-ree'uh-fil-ip'*i*, ses'uh-ree'uh-fil'i-p*i*
Caiaphas	kay'uh-fuhs
Cain	kayn
Cainan	kay'nuhn
Calah	kay'luh
Calamolalus	kal'uh-mol'uh-luhs
calamus	kal'uh-muhs
Calcol	kal'kol
Caleb	kay'luhb
Caleb-ephratah	kay'luhb-ef'ruh-tuh
Caleb-ephrathah	kay'luhb-ef'ruh-thuh
Caleb Ephrathah	kay'luhb-ef'ruh-thuh
Calebite	kay'luh-b*i*t
Calitas	kuh-l*i*"tuhs
Callisthenes	kuh-lis'thuh-neez
Calneh	kal'neh
Calno	kal'noh
Calvary	kal'vuh-ree
Camon	kay'muhn
camphire	kam'f*i*r
Cana	kay'nuh
Canaan	kay'nuhn
Canaanite	kay'nuh-n*i*t
Canaanitess	kay'nuh-n*i*t-es
Canaanitish	kay'nuh-n*i*t-ish
Cananaean	kay'nuh-nee'uhn
Candace	kan'duh-see
Canneh	kan'uh
Canticle	kan'ti-kuhl
Capernaum	kuh-puhr'nay-uhm
Cape-salmone	kayp'sal-moh'nee
caph	kahf
Capharnaum	kuh-fahr'nay-uhm
Capharsalama	kaf'uhr-sal'uh-muh
Caphar-salama	kaf'uhr-sal'uh-muh
Caphenatha	kuh-fen'uh-thuh
Caphira	kuh-f*i*"ruh
Caphirim	kuh-f*i*"rim
Caphthorim	kaf'thuh-rim
Caphtor	kaf'tor
Caphtorim	kaf'tuh-rim
Caphtorite	kaf'tuh-r*i*t

---

a cat, ah father, ahr lard, air care, aw jaw, ay pay, b bug, ch chew, d do,
e, eh pet, ee seem, er error, f fun, g good, h hot, hw whether, i it, *i* sky,
ihr ear, j joke, k king, kh ch as in German *Buch*, ks vex, kw quill, l love, m mat,

Cappadocia	kap'uh-doh'shee-uh
Car	kahr
Carabasion	kair'uh-bay'zhee-uhn
Carcas	kahr'kuhs
Carchamis	kahr'kuh-mis
Carchemish	kahr'kuh-mish
Careah	kuh-ree'uh
Carem	kair'uhm
Caria	kair'ee-uh
Carian	kair'ee-uhn
Carite	kair'it
Carkas	kahr'kuhs
Carmanian	kahr-may'nee-uhn
Carme	kahr'mee
Carmel	kahr'muhl
Carmelite	kahr'muh-lit
Carmelitess	kahr'muh-lit-es
Carmi	kahr'mi
Carmite	kahr'mit
Carmonian	kahr-moh'nee-uhn
Carnaim	kahr-nay'im
Carnion	kahr'nee-uhn
Carpus	kahr'puhs
Carshena	kahr-shee'nuh
Casiphia	kuh-sif'ee-uh
Casleu	kas'loo
Casluh	kas'luh
Casluhim	kas'luh-him
Casluhite	kas'luh-hit
Casphor	kas'for
Caspin	kas'pin
cassia	kash'uh
Castor	kas'tuhr
Cathua	kuh-thoo'uh
Cauda	kaw'duh
Cedemite	ked'uh-mit
Cedron	see'druhn
Ceilan	see'luhn
Celosyria	see'loh-sihr'ee-uh
Cenchrea	sen'kree-uh
Cenchreae	sen'kruh-ee
Cendebaeus	sen'duh-bee'uhs
Cendebeus	sen'duh-bee'uhs
centurion	sen-tyoor'ee-uhn
Cephas	see'fuhs

n not, ng sing, o hot, oh go, oi boy, oo foot, *oo* boot, oor poor, or for,
ou how, p pat, r run, s so, sh sure, t toe, th thin, *th* then, ts tsetse,
tw twin, uh ago, uhr her, v vow, w weather, y young, z zone, zh vision

Cesar	see'zuhr
Cesarea	ses'uh-ree'uh
Cetab	see'tab
Chabod	kah-bohd'
Chabris	kab'ris
Chadias	kay'dee-uhs
Chadiasan	kay'dee-ay'shuhn
Chaereas	kihr'ee-uhs
chalcedony	kal-sed'uh-nee
Chalcol	kal'kol
Chaldaea	kal-dee'uh
Chaldaean	kal-dee'uhn
Chaldea	kal-dee'uh
Chaldean	kal-dee'uhn
Chaldee	kal-dee'
Chalphi	kal'f*i*
Cham	kam
Chanaan	kay'nuhn
Channuneus	kan'uh-nee'uhs
Chaphenatha	kuh-fen'uh-thuh
Charaathalar	kair'ay-ath'uh-lahr
Characa	kair'uh-kuh
Charashim	kair'uh-shim
Charax	kair'aks
Charchamis	kahr'kuh-mis
Charchemish	kahr'kuh-mish
Charcus	kahr'kuhs
Charea	kair'ee-uh
Charmis	kahr'mis
Charran	kair'uhn
Chaseba	kas'uh-buh
Chaspho	kas'foh
Chebar	kee'bahr
Chedorlaomer	ked'uhr-lay-oh'muhr
Chelal	kee'lal
Chelcias	kel'shee-uhs
Cheleoud	kel'ee-*oo*d
Chellean	kel'ee-uhn
Chellian	kel'ee-uhn
Chelluh	kel'uh
Chellus	kel'uhs
Chelod	kee'lod
Chelous	kel'uhs
Chelub	kee'luhb
Chelubai	ki-l*oo*'b*i*

a cat, ah father, ahr lard, air care, aw jaw, ay pay, b bug, ch chew, d do,
e, eh pet, ee seem, er error, f fun, g good, h hot, hw whether, i it, *i* sky,
ihr ear, j joke, k king, kh ch as in German Buch, ks vex, kw quill, l love, m mat,

Cheluh	kel′uh
Cheluhi	kel′uh-h*i*
Chemarim	kem′uh-rim
Chemosh	kee′mosh
Chenaanah	ki-nay′uh-nuh
Chenani	ki-nay′n*i*
Chenaniah	ken′uh-n*i*′uh
Chepharammoni	kee′fuhr-am′uh-n*i*
Chephar-ammoni	kee′fuhr-am′uh-n*i*
Chephar-haammonai	kee′fuhr-hay-am′uh-n*i*
Chephar Haammoni	kee′fuhr-hay-am′uh-n*i*
Chephirah	ki-f*i*′ruh
Chephirim	kef′uh-rim
Cheran	kihr′uhn
Chereas	kihr′ee-uhs
Cherethim	ker′uh-thim
Cherethite	ker′uh-th*i*t
Cherith	ker′ith
Cherub	ker′uhb
cherub	cher′uhb
cherubim	cher′uh-bim
Chesalon	kes′uh-lon
Chesed	kee′sed
Chesil	kee′suhl
Chesulloth	ki-suhl′oth
cheth	keth
Chettiim	ket′uh-im
Chezib	kee′zib
Chidon	k*i*′duhn
Chileab	kil′ee-ab
Chilion	kil′ee-uhn
Chilmad	kil′mad
Chimham	kim′ham
Chinnereth	kin′uh-reth
Chinneroth	kin′uh-roth
Chios	k*i*′os
Chisleu	kiz′l*oo*
Chislev	kiz′lev
Chislon	kiz′lon
Chislothtabor	kiz′loth-tay′buhr
Chisloth-tabor	kiz′loth-tay′buhr
Chisloth Tabor	kiz′loth-tay′buhr
Chitlish	kit′lish
Chittim	kit′im
Chiun	k*i*′uhn

n not, ng sing, o hot, oh go, oi boy, oo foot, *oo* boot, oor poor, or for, ou how, p pat, r run, s so, sh sure, t toe, th thin, *th* then, ts tsetse, tw twin, uh ago, uhr her, v vow, w weather, y young, z zone, zh vision

Chloe	kloh'ee
Choba	koh'buh
Chorashan	kor-ay'shuhn
Chor-ashan	kor-ay'shuhn
Chorazin	koh-ray'zin
Chorbe	kor'bee
Chosamaeus	kos'uh-mee'uhs
Chozeba	koh-zee'buh
Christ	kr*i*st
Christian	kris'chuhn
Chronicle	kron'i-kuhl
chrysoprase	kris'uh-prayz
chrysoprasus	kris'uh-pray'zuhs
Chub	kuhb
Chun	kuhn
Chushan-rishathaim	koo'shan-rish'uh-thay'im
Chusi	ky*oo*'s*i*
Chuza	ky*oo*'zuh
Cilicia	suh-lish'ee-uh
cincture	sink'chuhr
Cinneroth	sin'uh-roth
Cirama	suh-ray'muh
Cis	sis
Cisai	s*i*'s*i*
cithara	sith'uh-ruh
cithern	sith'uhrn
Citim	sit'im
Clauda	klaw'duh
Claudia	klaw'dee-uh
Claudius	klaw'dee-uhs
Clement	klem'uhnt
Cleopas	klee'oh-puhs
Cleopatra	klee'uh-pat'ruh
Cleophas	klee'oh-fuhs
Clopas	kloh'puhs
Cnidus	n*i*'duhs
Coelesyria	see'lee-sihr'ee-uh
Coele-syria	see'lee-sihr'ee-uh
Col	kol
Cola	koh'luh
Colhozeh	kol-hoh'zuh
Col-hozeh	kol-hoh'zuh
Colius	koh-l*i*'uhs
Colossae	kuh-los'ee
Colosse	kuh-los'ee

a cat, ah father, ahr lard, air care, aw jaw, ay pay, b bug, ch chew, d do,
e, eh pet, ee seem, er error, f fun, g good, h hot, hw whether, i it, *i* sky,
ihr ear, j joke, k king, kh ch as in German Buch, ks vex, kw quill, l love, m mat,

Colossian	kuh-losh'uhn
Comforter	kuhm'for-tuhr
Commentary	kom'en-ter-ee
Conaniah	kon'uh-n*i*'uh
Coniah	koh-n*i*'uh
Cononiah	kon'uh-n*i*'uh
consul	kon'suhl
Coos	koh'os
cor	kor
Corashan	kor-ash'uhn
corban	kor'ban
Corbe	kor'bee
Core	koh'ree
Corinth	kor'inth
Corinthian	kuh-rin'thee-uhn
Corinthus	kuh-rin'thuhs
Cornelius	kor-neel'yuhs
Cos	kos
Cosam	koh'suhm
coulter	kohl'tuhr
Council	koun'suhl
Counseller	koun'suh-luhr
Counsellor	koun'suh-luhr
Counselor	koun'suh-luhr
Coutha	koo'thuh
Covenant	kuhv'uh-nuhnt
Covenant-box	kuhv'uh-nuhnt-boks'
Covenant-tent	kuhv'uh-nuhnt-tent'
Coz	koz
Cozbi	koz'b*i*
Cozeba	koh-zee'buh
Crates	kray'teez
Creator	kree-ay'tuhr
Crescens	kres'uhnz
Cretan	kree'tuhn
Crete	kreet
Cretian	kree'shuhn
Crispus	kris'puhs
Cub	kuhb
cubit	ky*oo*'bit
Culom	k*oo*'luhm
Culon	k*oo*'luhn
cumi	ky*oo*'mee
cumin	kuh'min
cummin	kuh'min

n not, ng sing, o hot, oh go, oi boy, oo foot, *oo* boot, oor poor, or for,
ou how, p pat, r run, s so, sh sure, t toe, th thin, *th* then, ts tsetse,
tw twin, uh ago, uhr her, v vow, w weather, y young, z zone, zh vision

Cun	kuhn
Cush	koosh
Cushan	koosh'an
Cushanrishathaim	koosh'an-rish'uh-thay'im
Cushan-rishathaim	koosh'an-rish'uh-thay'im
Cushi	koosh'*i*
Cushite	koosh'*i*t
Cuth	kooth
Cutha	kooth'uh
Cuthah	kooth'uh
Cuza	k*oo*'zuh
Cyamon	s*i*'uh-muhn
Cyaxares	s*i*-aks'uh-reez
Cyprian	sip'ree-uhn
Cypriot	sip'ree-uht
Cyprus	s*i*'pruhs
Cyrene	s*i*-ree'nee
Cyrenean	s*i*-ree'nee-uhn
Cyreni	s*i*-ree'nee
Cyrenian	s*i*-ree'nee-uhn
Cyrenius	s*i*-ree'nee-uhs
Cyrus	s*i*'ruhs

D

Dabareh	dab'uh-ruh
Dabbasheth	dab'uh-sheth
Dabbesheth	dab'uh-sheth
Daberath	dab'uh-rath
Dabria	dab'ree-uh
Dacobi	day'kuh-b*i*
Daddeus	dad'ee-uhs
Dadu	day'd*oo*
Dagon	day'gon
Daisan	day'suhn
Dalaiah	duh-lay'yuh
daleth	dah'leth
Dalila	duh-l*i*'luh
Dalmanutha	dal'muh-n*oo*'thuh
Dalmatia	dal-may'shee-uh
Dalphon	dal'fon

a cat, ah father, ahr lard, air care, aw jaw, ay pay, b bug, ch chew, d do,
e, eh pet, ee seem, er error, f fun, g good, h hot, hw whether, i it, *i* sky,
ihr ear, j joke, k king, kh ch as in German *Buch*, ks vex, kw quill, l love, m mat,

Damaris	dam′uh-ris
Damascene	dam′uh-seen
Damascus	duh-mas′kuhs
Dammin	dam′in
Dan	dan
Daniel	dan′yuhl
Danite	dan′it
Dan-jaan	dan-jay′uhn
Dan Jaan	dan-jay′uhn
Dannah	dan′uh
Daphne	daf′nee
Dara	dair′uh
Darda	dahr′duh
daric	dair′ik
Darius	duh-ri′uhs
Darkon	dahr′kon
Dathan	day′thuhn
Dathema	dath′uh-muh
David	day′vid
daysman	dayz′muhn
Daystar	day′stahr
Day-star	day′stahr
Day Star	day′stahr
deacon	dee′kuhn
deaconess	dee′kuh-nis
Dead Sea	ded-see′
Debar	dee′buhr
Debarim	dee′buh-rim
Debir	dee′buhr
Debora	deb′uh-ruh
Deborah	deb′uh-ruh
Decapolis	di-kap′uh-lis
Decision	di-sizh′uhn
Dedan	dee′duhn
Dedanim	dee′duh-nim
Dedanite	dee′duh-nit
Dehavite	di-hay′vit
Deity	dee′uh-tee
Dekar	dee′kuhr
Deker	dee′kuhr
Delaiah	di-lay′yuh
Delilah	di-li′luh
Delos	dee′los
Delus	dee′luhs
Demas	dee′muhs

---

n not, ng sing, o hot, oh go, oi boy, oo foot, *oo* boot, oor poor, or for,
ou how, p pat, r run, s so, sh sure, t toe, th thin, *th* then, ts tsetse,
tw twin, uh ago, uhr her, v vow, w weather, y young, z zone, zh vision

Demetrius	di-mee'tree-uhs
demoniac	di-moh'nee-ak
Demophon	dem'uh-fon
denarii	di-nair'ee-*i*
denarius	di-nair'ee-uhs
Derbe	duhr'bee
Desolating Sacrilege	des'oh-lay-ting-sak'ruh-lij
Dessau	des'aw
Deuel	d*oo*'uhl
Deuteronomy	d*oo*'tuh-ron'uh-mee
Devil	dev'uhl
Diana	d*i*-an'uh
Diaspora	d*i*-as'puh-ruh
Diblah	dib'luh
Diblaim	dib'lay-im
Diblath	dib'lath
Diblathaim	dib'luh-thay'im
Dibon	d*i*'bon
Dibongad	d*i*'bon-gad'
Dibon-gad	d*i*'bon-gad'
Dibon Gad	d*i*'bon-gad'
Dibri	dib'r*i*
Didymus	did'uh-muhs
Diklah	dik'luh
Dilean	dil'ee-uhn
Dimnah	dim'nuh
Dimon	d*i*'muhn
Dimonah	di-moh'nuh
Dinah	d*i*'nuh
Dinaite	d*i*'nay-*i*t
Dinhabah	din'huh-buh
Dionysius	d*i*'uh-nish'ee-uhs
Dionysus	d*i*'uh-n*i*'suhs
Dioscorinthius	d*i*'uhs-kuh-rin'thee-uhs
Diotrephes	d*i*-ot'ruh-feez
Diphath	d*i*'fath
disciple	di-s*i*'puhl
Dishan	d*i*'shan
Dishon	d*i*'shon
Dispersion	dis-puhr'zhuhn
Dizahab	diz'uh-hab
Docus	doh'kuhs
Dodai	doh'd*i*
Dodanim	doh'duh-nim
Dodavah	doh'duh-vuh

---

a cat, ah father, ahr lard, air care, aw jaw, ay pay, b bug, ch chew, d do,
e, eh pet, ee seem, er error, f fun, g good, h hot, hw whether, i it, *i* sky,
ihr ear, j joke, k king, kh ch as in German *Buch*, ks vex, kw quill, l love, m mat,

Dodavahu	doh'duh-vay'hy*oo*
Dodavhu	doh-dav'hy*oo*
Dodo	doh'doh
Doeg	doh'ig
Dok	dok
Dophkah	dof'kuh
Dor	dor
Dora	dor'uh
Dorcas	dor'kuhs
Dorymenes	dor-im'uh-neez
Dositheus	doh-sith'ee-uhs
Dothaim	doh'thay-im
Dothan	doh'thuhn
drachma	drak'muh
dram	dram
Drimylus	drim'uh-luhs
Drusilla	dr*oo*-sil'uh
Dumah	d*oo*'muh
Dura	door'uh

E

Eanes	ee'uh-neez
Easter	ee'stuhr
Ebal	ee'buhl
Ebed	ee'bid
Ebedmelech	ee'bid-mee'lik
Ebed-melech	ee'bid-mee'lik
Eben-bohan-ben-reuben	ee'ben-boh'han-ben-r*oo*'ben
Ebenezer	eb'uh-nee'zuhr
Eber	ee'buhr
Ebez	ee'biz
Ebiasaph	i-b*i*'uh-saf
Ebron	ee'bruhn
Ebronah	i-broh'nuh
Ecanus	i-kay'nuhs
Ecbatana	ek-bat'uh-nuh
Ecclesiastes	i-klee'zee-as'teez
Ecclesiasticus	i-klee'zee-as'ti-kuhs
Ed	ed
Edar	ee'duhr

n not, ng sing, o hot, oh go, oi boy, oo foot, *oo* boot, oor poor, or for,
ou how, p pat, r run, s so, sh sure, t toe, th thin, *th* then, ts tsetse,
tw twin, uh ago, uhr her, v vow, w weather, y young, z zone, zh vision

Eddias	i-di'uhs
Eddinus	ed'uh-nuhs
Eden	ee'duhn
Edenite	ee'duh-nit
Eder	ee'duhr
Edes	ee'deez
Edna	ed'nuh
Edom	ee'duhm
Edomite	ee'duh-mit
Edrei	ed'ree-i
Eglah	eg'luh
Eglaim	eg'lay-im
Eglathshelishiyah	eg'lath-shi-lish'uh-yuh
Eglath-shelishiyah	eg'lath-shi-lish'uh-yuh
Eglath Shelishiyah	eg'lath-shi-lish'uh-yuh
Eglon	eg'lon
Egrebel	i-gree'buhl
Egypt	ee'jipt
Egyptian	i-jip'shuhn
Ehi	ee'hi
Ehud	ee'huhd
Ekah	ee'kuh
Eker	ee'kuhr
Ekrebel	ek'ruh-buhl
Ekron	ek'ruhn
Ekronite	ek'ruh-nit
El	el
Ela	ee'luh
Eladah	el'uh-duh
Elah	ee'luh
Elam	ee'luhm
Elamite	ee'luh-mit
Elasa	el'uh-suh
Elasah	el'uh-suh
Elath	ee'lath
Elberith	el'bi-rith'
El-berith	el'bi-rith'
Elbethel	el-beth'uhl
El-bethel	el-beth'uhl
El-beth-el	el-beth'uhl
El Bethel	el-beth'uhl
Elcia	el-ki'uh
Eldaah	el-day'uh
Eldad	el'dad
Elead	el'ee-uhd

a cat, ah father, ahr lard, air care, aw jaw, ay pay, b bug, ch chew, d do,
e, eh pet, ee seem, er error, f fun, g good, h hot, hw whether, i it, i sky,
ihr ear, j joke, k king, kh ch as in German Buch, ks vex, kw quill, l love, m mat,

Eleadah	el'ee-ay'duh
Elealeh	el'ee-ay'luh
Eleasa	el'ee-ay'suh
Eleasah	el'ee-ay'suh
Eleazar	el'ee-ay'zuhr
Eleazurus	el'ee-uh-zoor'uhs
El-elohe-israel	el-el'oh-heh-is'ray-uhl
El Elohe Israel	el-el'oh-heh-is'ray-uhl
El-elyon	el'el-yohn'
El Elyon	el'el-yohn'
Eleph	ee'lif
Eleutherus	i-loo'thuh-ruhs
Elhanan	el-hay'nuhn
Eli	ee'li
Eliab	i-li'uhb
Eliaba	i-li'uh-buh
Eliada	i-li'uh-duh
Eliadah	i-li'uh-duh
Eliadas	i-li'uh-duhs
Eliadun	i-li'uh-duhn
Eliah	i-li'uh
Eliakim	i-li'uh-kim
Eliali	i-li'uh-li
Elialis	i-li'uh-lis
Eliam	i-li'uhm
Eliaonias	i-li'uh-oh-ni'uhs
Elias	i-li'uhs
Eliasaph	i-li'uh-saf
Eliashib	i-li'uh-shib
Eliasib	i-li'uh-sib
Eliasis	i-li'uh-sis
Eliathah	i-li'uh-thuh
Elidad	i-li'dad
Eliehoenai	i-li'uh-hoh-ee'ni
Eliel	i-li'uhl
Eli-Eli-lama-sabachthani	ee'li-ee'li-lah'muh-suh-bahk'thuh-nee
Eli Eli lama sabachthani	ee'li-ee'li-lah'muh-suh-bahk'thuh-nee
Eli Eli lama sabach-thani	ee'li-ee'li-lah'muh-suh-bahk'thuh-nee
Elienai	el'ee-ee'ni
Eliezar	el'ee-ee'zuhr
Eliezer	el'ee-ee'zuhr
Elihoenai	el'ee-hoh-ee'ni
Elihoreph	el'uh-hoh'rif
Elihu	i-li'hyoo
Elijah	i-li'juh

n not, ng sing, o hot, oh go, oi boy, oo foot, oo boot, oor poor, or for,
ou how, p pat, r run, s so, sh sure, t toe, th thin, th then, ts tsetse,
tw twin, uh ago, uhr her, v vow, w weather, y young, z zone, zh vision

Elika	i-l*i*″kuh
Elim	ee′lim
Elimelech	i-lim′uh-lek
Elioenai	el′ee-oh-ee′n*i*
Elionas	el′ee-oh′nuhs
Eliphal	i-l*i*″fuhl
Eliphalat	i-lif′uh-lat
Eliphalet	i-lif′uh-let
Eliphaz	el′i-faz
Elipheleh	i-lif′uh-luh
Eliphelehu	i-lif′uh-lee′hy*oo*
Eliphelet	i-lif′uh-let
Elipheleth	i-lif′uh-leth
Elisabeth	i-liz′uh-buhht
Elisaeus	el′uh-see′uhs
Eliseus	el′uh-see′uhs
Elisha	i-l*i*″shuh
Elishah	i-l*i*″shuh
Elishama	i-lish′uh-muh
Elishaphat	i-lish′uh-fat
Elisheba	i-lish′uh-buh
Elishua	el′uh-sh*oo*′uh
Elisimus	i-lis′i-muhs
Elite	ee′l*i*t
Eliu	i-l*i*″y*oo*
Eliud	i-l*i*″uhd
Elizabeth	i-liz′uh-buhht
Elizaphan	el′uh-zay′fan
Elizur	i-l*i*″zuhr
Eljehoenai	el′juh-hoh-ee′n*i*
Elkanah	el-kay′nuh
Elkesh	el′kesh
Elkiah	el-k*i*′uh
Elkohshite	el′koh-sh*i*t
Elkosh	el′kosh
Elkoshite	el′kosh-*i*t
Ellasar	el′uh-sahr
Elmadam	el-may′duhm
Elmodam	el-moh′duhm
Elnaam	el-nay′uhm
Elnathan	el-nay′thuhn
Eloah	i-loh′uh
Elohe	el-oh′heh
Eloi	ee′loh-*i*

---

a cat, ah father, ahr lard, air care, aw jaw, ay pay, b bug, ch chew, d do,
e, eh pet, ee seem, er error, f fun, g good, h hot, hw whether, i it, *i* sky,
ihr ear, j joke, k king, kh ch as in German *Buch*, ks vex, kw quill, l love, m mat,

Elo-i Elo-i lama sabach-thani	ee'loh-*i*-ee'loh-*i*-lah'muh-suh-bahk' thuh-nee
Elon	ee'lon
Elonbethhanan	ee'luhn-beth-hay'nuhn
Elonbeth-hanan	ee'luhn-beth-hay'nuhn
Elon-beth-hanan	ee'luhn-beth-hay'nuhn
Elon Bethhanan	ee'luhn-beth-hay'nuhn
Elon Beth Hanan	ee'luhn-beth-hay'nuhn
Elonite	ee'luh-n*i*t
Elon-meonenim	ee'luhn-mee-on'uh-nim
Eloth	ee'loth
Elpaal	el-pay'uhl
Elpalet	el-pay'lit
Elparan	el-pay'ruhn
El-paran	el-pay'ruhn
El Paran	el-pay'ruhn
Elpelet	el-pee'lit
Elteke	el'tuh-kuh
Eltekeh	el'tuh-kuh
Eltekoh	el'tuh-koh
Eltekon	el'tuh-kon
Eltolad	el-toh'lad
Elul	ee'luhl
Eluzai	i-*loo*'z*i*
Elymaean	el'uh-mee'uhn
Elymais	el'uh-may'uhs
Elymas	el'uh-muhs
Elzabad	el-zay'bad
Elzaphan	el-zay'fan
Emadabun	i-mad'uh-buhn
Emath	ee'math
Emathis	em'uh-thuhs
Emek	ee'mik
Emekkeziz	ee'mik-kee'ziz
Emek-keziz	ee'mik-kee'ziz
Emek Keziz	ee'mik-kee'ziz
emerod	em'uh-rod
Emim	ee'mim
Emite	ee'm*i*t
Emmanuel	i-man'y*oo*-uhl
Emmaus	i-may'uhs
Emmer	em'uhr
Emmor	em'or
En	en
Enac	ee'nak

---

n **not**, ng **sing**, o **hot**, oh **go**, oi **boy**, oo **foot**, *oo* **boot**, oor **poor**, or **for**, ou **how**, p **pat**, r **run**, s **so**, sh **sure**, t **toe**, th **thin**, *th* **then**, ts **tsetse**, tw **twin**, uh **ago**, uhr **her**, v **vow**, w **weather**, y **young**, z **zone**, zh **vision**

Enaim	i-nay'im
Enam	ee'nuhm
Enan	ee'nuhn
Enasibus	i-nas'uh-buhs
Endor	en'dor
En-dor	en'dor
En Dor	en'dor
Eneas	i-nee'uhs
Eneglaim	en-eg'lay-im
En-eglaim	en-eg'lay-im
En Eglaim	en-eg'lay-im
Enemessar	en'uh-mes'uhr
Enenius	i-nen'ee-uhs
Engaddi	en-gad'*i*
Engannim	en-gan'im
En-gannim	en-gan'im
En Gannim	en-gan'im
Engedi	en-ged'*i*
En-gedi	en-ged'*i*
En Gedi	en-ged'*i*
Enhaddah	en-had'uh
En-haddah	en-had'uh
En Haddah	en-had'uh
Enhakkore	en-hak'uh-ree
En-hakkore	en-hak'uh-ree
En Hakkore	en-hak'uh-ree
En-harod	en-hair'od
Enhazor	en-hay'zor
En-hazor	en-hay'zor
En Hazor	en-hay'zor
Enmishpat	en-mish'pat
En-mishpat	en-mish'pat
En Mishpat	en-mish'pat
Ennom	en'uhm
Enoch	ee'nuhk
Enon	ee'nuhn
Enon-City	ee'nuhn-sit'ee
Enos	ee'nuhs
Enosh	ee'nosh
Enrimmon	en-rim'uhn
En-rimmon	en-rim'uhn
En Rimmon	en-rim'uhn
Enrogel	en-roh'guhl
En-rogel	en-roh'guhl
En Rogel	en-roh'guhl

a cat, ah father, ahr lard, air care, aw jaw, ay pay, b bug, ch chew, d do,
e, eh pet, ee seem, er error, f fun, g good, h hot, hw whether, i it, *i* sky,
ihr ear, j joke, k king, kh ch as in German Buch, ks vex, kw quill, l love, m mat,

Enshemesh	en-shem'ish
En-shemesh	en-shem'ish
En Shemesh	en-shem'ish
Entappuah	en-tap'y*oo*-uh
En-tappuah	en-tap'y*oo*-uh
En Tappuah	en-tap'y*oo*-uh
Epaenetus	i-pee'nuh-tuhs
Epaphras	ep'uh-fras
Epaphroditus	i-paf'ruh-d*i*'tuhs
Epeiph	ee'f*i*f
Epenetus	i-pee'nuh-tuhs
Ephah	ee'fuh
ephah	ee'fuh
Ephai	ee'f*i*
Epher	ee'fuhr
Ephesdammim	ee'fiz-dam'im
Ephes-dammim	ee'fiz-dam'im
Ephes Dammim	ee'fiz-dam'im
Ephes-dammin	ee'fiz-dam'in
Ephesian	i-fee'zhuhn
Ephesus	ef'uh-suhs
Ephlal	ef'lal
Ephod	ee'fod
ephod	ee'fod
ephphatha	ef'uh-thuh
Ephraim	ee'fray-im
Ephraimite	ee'fray-uh-m*i*t
Ephrain	ee'fray-in
Ephratah	ef'ruh-tuh
Ephrath	ef'rath
Ephrathah	ef'ruh-thuh
Ephrathite	ef'ruh-th*i*t
Ephron	ee'fron
Epicurean	ep'i-kyoo-ree'uhn
Epiphanes	i-pif'uh-neez
Epiphi	ep'i-f*i*
Epistle	i-pis'uhl
Er	uhr
Eran	ihr'an
Eranite	ihr'uh-n*i*t
Erastus	i-ras'tuhs
Erech	ee'rik
Eri	ee'r*i*
Erite	ee'r*i*t
Esaias	i-zay'yuhs

n not, ng sing, o hot, oh go, oi boy, oo foot, *oo* boot, oor poor, or for,
ou how, p pat, r run, s so, sh sure, t toe, th thin, *th* then, ts tsetse,
tw twin, uh ago, uhr her, v vow, w weather, y young, z zone, zh vision

Esarhaddon	ee'suhr-had'uhn
Esar-haddon	ee'suhr-had'uhn
Esau	ee'saw
Esdraelon	ez'druh-ee'luhn
Esdras	ez'druhs
Esdris	ez'dris
Esebon	es'i-bon
Esebrias	es'i-br*i*'uhs
Esek	ee'sik
Eshan	ee'shuhn
Eshbaal	esh-bay'uhl
Esh-baal	esh-bay'uhl
Eshban	esh'ban
Esh-ban	esh'ban
Eshcol	esh'kol
Eshean	esh'ee-uhn
Eshek	ee'shik
Eshkalonite	esh'kuh-luh-n*i*t
Eshtaol	esh'tay-uhl
Eshtaolite	esh'tay-uh-l*i*t
Eshtarah	esh'tuh-ruh
Eshtaulite	esh'tuh-y*oo*'l*i*t
Eshtemoa	esh'tuh-moh'uh
Eshtemoh	esh'tuh-moh
Eshton	esh'ton
Esli	es'l*i*
Esora	i-sor'uh
Esril	es'ril
Esrom	es'rom
Ester	es'tuhr
Esther	es'tuhr
Etam	ee'tuhm
Etham	ee'thuhm
Ethan	ee'thuhn
Ethanim	eth'uh-nim
Ethanus	i'thay'nuhs
Ethbaal	eth-bay'uhl
Ether	ee'thuhr
Ethiopia	ee'thee-oh'pee-uh
Ethiopian	ee'thee-oh'pee-uhn
Ethkazin	eth-kay'zin
Eth-kazin	eth-kay'zin
Eth Kazin	eth-kay'zin
Ethma	eth'muh
Ethnan	eth'nuhn

---

a cat, ah father, ahr lard, air care, aw jaw, ay pay, b bug, ch chew, d do,
e, eh pet, ee seem, er error, f fun, g good, h hot, hw whether, i it, *i* sky,
ihr ear, j joke, k king, kh ch as in German *Buch*, ks vex, kw quill, l love, m mat,

ethnarch	eth'nahrk
Ethni	eth'n*i*
Eubulus	y*oo*-by*oo*'luhs
Euergetes	y*oo*-uhr'juh-teez
Eumenes	y*oo*'muh-neez
Eunatan	y*oo*-nay'tuhn
Eunice	y*oo*'nis
eunuch	y*oo*'nuhk
Euodia	y*oo*-oh'dee-uh
Euodias	y*oo*-oh'dee-uhs
Eupator	y*oo*'puh-tor
Euphrates	y*oo*-fray'teez
Eupolemus	y*oo*-pol'uh-muhs
Eurakylon	y*oo*-rahk'i-lon
Euraquila	y*oo*-rahk'wi-luh
Euraquilo	y*oo*-rahk'wi-loh
Euroclydon	y*oo*-rok'li-don
Eutychus	y*oo*'tuh-kuhs
Evangelist	i-van'juh-list
Eve	eev
Evi	ee'v*i*
Evilmerodach	ee'vuhl-mer'uh-dak
Evil-merodach	ee'vuhl-mer'uh-dak
Evodia	i-voh'dee-uh
Exodus	ek'suh-duhs
Ezar	ee'zuhr
Ezbai	ez'b*i*
Ezbon	ez'bon
Ezechias	ez'uh-k*i*'uhs
Ezechiel	i-zee'kee-uhl
Ezecias	ez'uh-k*i*'uhs
Ezekias	ez'uh-k*i*'uhs
Ezekiel	i-zee'kee-uhl
Ezel	ee'zuhl
Ezem	ee'zuhm
Ezer	ee'zuhr
Ezerias	ez'uh-r*i*'uhs
Ezias	i-z*i*'uhs
Ezion-gaber	ee'zee-uhn-gay'buhr
Eziongeber	ee'zee-uhn-gee'buhr
Ezion-geber	ee'zee-uhn-gee'buhr
Ezion Geber	ee'zee-uhn-gee'buhr
Eznite	ez'n*i*t
Ezora	i-zor'uh
Ezra	ez'ruh

n **n**ot, ng si**ng**, o h**o**t, oh g**o**, oi b**oy**, oo f**oo**t, *oo* b**oo**t, oor p**oor**, or f**or**,
ou h**ow**, p **p**at, r **r**un, s **s**o, sh **s**ure, t **t**oe, th **th**in, *th* **th**en, ts **ts**etse,
tw **tw**in, uh **a**go, uhr h**er**, v **v**ow, w **w**eather, y **y**oung, z **z**one, zh vi**si**on

Ezrah	ez'ruh
Ezrahite	ez'ruh-hit
Ezra-Nehemyah	ez'ruh-ni-hem'yuh
Ezri	ez'ri
Ezrite	ez'rit

F

Fair-Havens	fair'hay'vinz
Fair Havens	fair'hay'vinz
farthing	fahr'thing
fauchion	faw'chuhn
Felix	fee'liks
felloe	fel'oh
Festus	fes'tuhs
firkin	fuhr'kin
Fortunatus	for'chuh-nay'tuhs
Forum of Appius	for'uhm-uhv-ap'ee-uhs

G

Gaal	gay'uhl
Gaash	gay'ash
Gaba	gay'buh
Gabael	gab'ay-uhl
Gabaon	gab'ay-uhn
Gabatha	gab'uh-thuh
Gabbai	gab'i
Gabbatha	gab'uh-thuh
Gabdes	gab'deez
Gaber	gay'buhr
Gaboes	gay'bohz
Gabri	gay'bri
Gabrias	gay'bree-uhs
Gabriel	gay'bree-uhl
Gad	gad
Gadara	gad'uh-ruh

---

a cat, ah father, ahr lard, air care, aw jaw, ay pay, b bug, ch chew, d do,
e, eh pet, ee seem, er error, f fun, g good, h hot, hw whether, i it, *i* sky,
ihr ear, j joke, k king, kh ch as in German *Buch*, ks vex, kw quill, l love, m mat,

Gadarene	gad'uh-reen
Gaddah	gad'uh
Gaddi	gad'*i*
Gaddiel	gad'ee-uhl
Gader	gay'duhr
Gadi	gay'd*i*
Gadite	gad'*i*t
Gaham	gay'ham
Gahar	gay'hahr
Gaher	gay'huhr
Gai	g*i*
Gaius	gay'yuhs
Galaad	gal'ay-uhd
Galal	gay'lal
Galatia	guh-lay'shuh
Galatian	guh-lay'shuhn
galbanum	gal'buh-nuhm
Galeed	gal'ee-ed
Galgal	gal'gal
Galgala	gal'guh-luh
Galilaean	gal'uh-lee'uhn
Galilean	gal'uh-lee'uhn
Galilee	gal'uh-lee
Gallim	gal'im
Gallio	gal'ee-oh
Gamad	gay'mad
Gamadite	gay'muh-d*i*t
Gamael	gam'ay-uhl
Gamaliel	guh-may'lee-uhl
Gammad	gam'uhd
Gammadim	gam'uh-dim
Gamul	gay'muhl
Gannim	gan'im
Gar	gahr
Gareb	gair'ib
Garizim	gair'uh-zim
Garmite	gahr'm*i*t
Gas	gas
Gashmu	gash'my*oo*
Gatam	gay'tuhm
Gath	gath
Gathhepher	gath-hee'fuhr
Gath-hepher	gath-hee'fuhr
Gath Hepher	gath-hee'fuhr
Gathrimmon	gath-rim'uhn

---

n **n**ot, ng si**ng**, o h**o**t, oh g**o**, oi b**oy**, oo f**oo**t, *oo* b**oo**t, oor p**oor**, or f**or**,
ou h**ow**, p **p**at, r **r**un, s **s**o, sh **s**ure, t **t**oe, th **th**in, *th* **th**en, ts **ts**etse,
tw **tw**in, uh **a**go, uhr h**er**, v **v**ow, w **w**eather, y **y**oung, z **z**one, zh vi**s**ion

Gath-rimmon	gath-rim'uhn
Gath Rimmon	gath-rim'uhn
Gaul	gawl
Gaulanitis	gawl'uh-ni'tis
Gaza	gay'zuh
Gazara	guh-zay'ruh
Gazathite	gay'zuh-thit
Gazer	gay'zuhr
Gazera	guh-zee'ruh
Gazez	gay'ziz
Gazite	gay'zit
Gazzam	gaz'uhm
Gazzan	gaz'uhn
Geba	gee'buh
Gebal	gee'buhl
Gebalite	gee'buh-lit
Geber	gee'buhr
Gebim	gee'bim
gecko	gek'oh
Gedaliah	ged'uh-li'uh
Geddur	ged'uhr
Gedeon	ged'ee-uhn
Geder	gee'duhr
Gederah	gi-dee'ruh
Gederathite	gi-dee'ruh-thit
Gederite	gi-dee'rit
Gederoth	gi-dee'roth
Gederothaim	gi-dee'ruh-thay'im
Gedi	ged'i
Gedor	gee'dor
Geharashim	gi-hair'uh-shim
Ge-harashim	gi-hair'uh-shim
Ge Harashim	gi-hair'uh-shim
Gehazi	gi-hay'zi
Gehenna	gi-hen'uh
Ge-hinnom	gi-hin'uhm
Gelboe	gel-boh'uh
Geliloth	gi-li'loth
Gemalli	gi-mal'i
Gemariah	gem'uh-ri'uh
Genesis	jen'uh-sis
Gennaeus	gi-nee'uhs
Gennesar	gi-nee'sahr
Gennesaret	gi-nes'uh-ret
Genneus	gi-nee'uhs

---

a cat, ah father, ahr lard, air care, aw jaw, ay pay, b bug, ch chew, d do,
e, eh pet, ee seem, er error, f fun, g good, h hot, hw whether, i it, i sky,
ihr ear, j joke, k king, kh ch as in German Buch, ks vex, kw quill, l love, m mat,

Gentile	jen't*i*l
Genubath	gi-ny*oo*'bath
Geon	gee'on
Gera	gee'ruh
Gerah	gee'ruh
gerah	gee'ruh
Gerar	gee'rahr
Gerasa	ger'uh-suh
Gerasene	ger'uh-seen
Gergesene	ger'guh-seen
Gergesite	ger'guh-s*i*t
Gerizim	ger'uh-zim
Geron	gihr'on
Gerrene	guh-ree'nee
Gerrhenian	guh-ree'nee-uhn
Gershom	guhr'shuhm
Gershomite	guhr'shuh-m*i*t
Gershon	guhr'shuhn
Gershonite	guhr'shuh-n*i*t
Gerson	guhr'suhn
Geruth Chimham	gihr'ooth-kim'ham
Geruth Kimham	gihr'ooth-kim'ham
Gerzite	guhr'z*i*t
Gesem	gee'suhm
Gesham	gee'shuhm
Geshan	gesh'uhn
Geshem	gesh'uhm
Geshur	gesh'uhr
Geshuri	gi-shoor'*i*
Geshurite	gesh'uh-r*i*t
Gessen	ges'uhn
Gether	gee'thuhr
Gethsemane	geth-sem'uh-nee
Geuel	gy*oo*'uhl
Gezer	gee'zuhr
Gezrite	gez'r*i*t
Giah	g*i*'uh
Gibbar	gib'ahr
Gibbeah	gib'ee-uh
Gibbeath	gib'ee-uhth
Gibbethon	gib'uh-thon
Gibea	gib'ee-uh
Gibeah	gib'ee-uh
Gibeath	gib'ee-uhth
Gibeathelohim	gib'ee-uhth-el'oh-him

n **not**, ng **sing**, o **hot**, oh **go**, oi **boy**, oo **foot**, *oo* **boot**, oor **poor**, or **for**,
ou **how**, p **pat**, r **run**, s **so**, sh **sure**, t **toe**, th **thin**, *th* **then**, ts **tsetse**,
tw **twin**, uh **ago**, uhr **her**, v **vow**, w **weather**, y **young**, z **zone**, zh **vision**

Gibeath-elohim	gib'ee-uhth-el'oh-him
Gibeath-haaraloth	gib'ee-uhth-hay-air'uh-loth
Gibeath-ha-araloth	gib'ee-uhth-hay-air'uh-loth
Gibeath Haaraloth	gib'ee-uhth-hay-air'uh-loth
Gibeath-hammoreh	gib'ee-uhth-hah-mor'uh
Gibeathite	gib'ee-uh-th*i*t
Gibeon	gib'ee-uhn
Gibeonite	gib'ee-uh-n*i*t
Giblite	gib'l*i*t
Giddalti	gi-dal't*i*
Giddel	gid'uhl
Gideon	gid'ee-uhn
Gideoni	gid'ee-oh'n*i*
Gidgad	gid'gad
Gidom	g*i*'duhm
gier	jihr
Giezi	g*i*-ee'z*i*
Gihon	g*i*'hon
Gilalai	gil'uh-l*i*
Gilboa	gil-boh'uh
Gilead	gil'ee-uhd
Gileadite	gil'ee-uh-d*i*t
Gilgal	gil'gal
Gilo	g*i*'loh
Giloh	g*i*'loh
Gilonite	g*i*'luh-n*i*t
gimel	gim'uhl
Gimzo	gim'zoh
Ginath	g*i*'nath
Ginnetho	gin'uh-thoh
Ginnethoi	gin'uh-thoi
Ginnethon	gin'uh-thon
Girgashite	guhr'guh-sh*i*t
Girgasite	guhr'guh-s*i*t
Girzite	guhr'z*i*t
Gishpa	gish'puh
Gispa	gis'puh
Gittah-hepher	git'uh-hee'fuhr
Gittaim	git'ay-im
Gittite	git'*i*t
Gittith	git'ith
Gizonite	g*i*'zoh-n*i*t
glede	gleed
Goah	goh'uh
Goath	goh'ath

---

a cat, ah father, ahr lard, air care, aw jaw, ay pay, b bug, ch chew, d do,
e, eh pet, ee seem, er error, f fun, g good, h hot, hw whether, i it, *i* sky,
ihr ear, j joke, k king, kh ch as in German *Buch*, ks vex, kw quill, l love, m mat,

Gob	gob
God	god
Godhead	god'hed
Gog	gog
Goiim	goi'im
Golan	goh'luhn
Golgotha	gol'guh-thuh
Goliath	guh-l*i*'uhth
Gomer	goh'muhr
Gomorrah	guh-mor'uh
Gomorrha	guh-mor'uh
Goren-ha-atad	gor'in-hah-ay'tad
Gorgias	gor'juhs
Gortyn	gor'tin
Gortyna	gor-t*i*'nuh
Goshen	goh'shuhn
Gospel	gos'puhl
Gotholiah	goth'uh-l*i*'uh
Gotholias	goth'uh-l*i*'uhs
Gothoniel	goh-thon'ee-uhl
Goyim	goi'im
Gozan	goh'zan
Gozen	goh'zuhn
Graba	grah'buh
Grecia	gree'shuh
Grecian	gree'shuhn
Greece	grees
Greek	greek
Gudgogah	gud-goh'duh
Guni	gy*oo*'n*i*
Gunite	gy*oo*-n*i*t
Gur	guhr
Gurbaal	guhr-bay'uhl
Gur-baal	guhr-bay'uhl
Gur Baal	guhr-bay'uhl

H

Haahashtari	hay'uh-hash'tuh-r*i*
Haammonai	hay-am'uh-n*i*
Habacuc	hab'uh-kuhk

---

n **n**ot, ng si**ng**, o h**o**t, oh g**o**, oi b**oy**, oo f**oo**t, *oo* b**oo**t, oor p**oor**, or f**or**,
ou h**ow**, p **p**at, r **r**un, s **s**o, sh **s**ure, t **t**oe, th **th**in, *th* **th**en, ts **ts**etse,
tw **tw**in, uh **a**go, uhr h**er**, v **v**ow, w **w**eather, y **y**oung, z **z**one, zh vi**s**ion

Habaiah	huh-bay'yuh
Habakkuk	huh-bak'uhk
Habaziniah	hab'uh-zi-n*i*'uh
Habazziniah	hab'uh-zi-n*i*'uh
Habbacuc	huh-bak'uhk
habergeon	hab'uhr-juhn
Habor	hay'bor
Habucuc	hab'uh-kuhk
Hacaliah	hak'uh-l*i*'uh
Haccerem	hak'uh-rem
Hachaliah	hak'uh-l*i*'uh
Hachamoni	hak'uh-moh'n*i*
Hachilah	huh-k*i*'luh
Hachmon	hak'muhn
Hachmoni	hak'moh-n*i*
Hachmonite	hak'moh-n*i*t
Hacmoni	hak'moh-n*i*
Hacmonite	hak'moh-n*i*t
Hadad	hay'dad
Hadadezer	hay'dad-ee'zuhr
Hadadrimmon	hay'dad-rim'uhn
Hadad Rimmon	hay'dad-rim'uhn
Hadar	hay'dahr
Hadarezer	hay'duhr-ee'zuhr
Hadashah	huh-dash'uh
Hadassah	huh-das'uh
Hadattah	huh-dat'uh
Haddah	had'uh
Haddon	had'uhn
Hades	hay'deez
Hadid	hay'did
Hadlai	had'l*i*
Hadoram	huh-dor'uhm
Hadrach	had'rak
Haeleph	hay-ee'lif
Hagab	hay'gab
Hagaba	hag'uh-buh
Hagabah	hag'uh-buh
Hagar	hay'gahr
Hagarene	hag'uh-reen
Hagarite	hag'uh-r*i*t
Hagerite	hay'gug-r*i*t
Haggadol	hag'uh-dol
Haggai	hag'*i*
Haggedolim	hag'uh-doh'lim

a cat, ah father, ahr lard, air care, aw jaw, ay pay, b bug, ch chew, d do,
e, eh pet, ee seem, er error, f fun, g good, h hot, hw whether, i it, *i* sky,
ihr ear, j joke, k king, kh ch as in German Buch, ks vex, kw quill, l love, m mat,

Haggeri	hag'uh-r*i*
Haggi	hag'ee
Haggiah	ha-g*i*'uh
Haggite	hag'*i*t
Haggith	hag'ith
Hagia	hay'gee-uh
Hagri	hag'r*i*
Hagrite	hag'r*i*t
Hahiroth	huh-h*i*'roth
Hai	h*i*
Hail	hayl
Hakeldama	huh-kel'duh-muh
Hakilah	huh-k*i*'luh
Hakkatan	hak'uh-tan
Hakkore	hak'uh-ree
Hakkoz	hak'oz
Hakupha	huh-ky*oo*'fuh
Halah	hay'luh
Halak	hay'lak
Halhul	hal'huhl
Hali	hay'l*i*
Halicarnassus	hal'uh-kahr-nas'uhs
hallel	hal'el
hallelujah	hal'uh-*loo*'yuh
Hallohesh	huh-loh'hesh
Halohesh	huh-loh'hesh
Ham	ham
Haman	hay'muhn
Hamath	hay'math
Hamathite	hay'muh-th*i*t
Hamathzobah	hay'math-zoh'buh
Hamath-zobah	hay'math-zoh'buh
Hamath Zobah	hay'math-zoh'buh
Hamite	ham'*i*t
Hammahlekoth	huh-mah'li-koth
Hammath	ham'ath
Hammedatha	ham'uh-day'thuh
Hammelech	ham'uh-lek
Hammolecheth	ha-mol'uh-keth
Hammoleketh	ha-mol'uh-keth
Hammon	ham'uhn
Hammothdor	ham'uhth-dor'
Hammoth-dor	ham'uhth-dor'
Hammoth Dor	ham'uhth-dor'
Hammuel	ham'y*oo*-uhl

---

n not, ng sing, o hot, oh go, oi boy, oo foot, *oo* boot, oor poor, or for,
ou how, p pat, r run, s so, sh sure, t toe, th thin, *th* then, ts tsetse,
tw twin, uh ago, uhr her, v vow, w weather, y young, z zone, zh vision

Hamon	hay′muhn
Hamonah	huh-moh′nuh
Hamongog	hay′muhn-gog′
Hamon-gog	hay′muhn-gog′
Hamon Gog	hay′muhn-gog′
Hamor	hay′mor
Hamran	ham′ran
Hamuel	ham′y*oo*-uhl
Hamul	hay′muhl
Hamulite	hay′muh-l*i*t
Hamutal	huh-my*oo*′tuhl
Hana	hay′nuh
Hanameel	huh-nam′ee-uhl
Hanamel	han′uh-mel
Hanan	hay′nuhn
Hananeal	huh-nan′ee-uhl
Hananeel	han′uh-neel
Hananel	han′uh-nel
Hanani	huh-nay′n*i*
Hananiah	han′uh-n*i*′uh
Hananiel	huh-nan′ee-uhl
Hanes	hay′neez
Haniel	han′ee-uhl
Hannah	han′uh
Hannathon	han′uh-thon
Hanniel	han′ee-uhl
Hanoch	hay′nok
Hanochite	hay′nuh-k*i*t
Hanun	hay′nuhn
Hapharaim	haf′uh-ray′im
Haphraim	haf-ray′im
Happizzez	hap′uh-zez
Happuch	hap′uhk
Hara	hair′uh
Haradah	huh-ray′duh
Haran	hair′uhn
Harar	hair′uhr
Hararite	hair′uh-r*i*t
Harbel	hahr′bel
Harbona	hahr-boh′nuh
Harbonah	hahr-boh′nuh
Harel	hair′uhl
Hareph	hair′if
Haresha	huh-ree′shuh
Hareth	hair′eth

---

a cat, ah father, ahr lard, air care, aw jaw, ay pay, b bug, ch chew, d do,
e, eh pet, ee seem, er error, f fun, g good, h hot, hw whether, i it, *i* sky,
ihr ear, j joke, k king, kh ch as in German *Buch*, ks vex, kw quill, l love, m mat,

Harhaiah	hahr-hay'yuh
Harhas	hahr'has
Harheres	hahr-hihr'iz
Har-heres	hahr-hihr'iz
Harhur	hahr'huhr
Harim	hair'im
Hariph	hair'if
Har-magedon	hahr'muh-ged'uhn
Harmon	hahr'muhn
Harnepher	hahr'nuh-fuhr
Harod	hair'uhd
Harodite	hair'uh-d*i*t
Haroeh	huh-roh'uh
Harorite	hay'roh-r*i*t
Harosheth	huh-roh'sheth
Harosheth Haggoyim	huh-roh'shith-huh-goi'im
Haroshethhagoiim	huh-roh'shith-huh-goi'im
Harosheth-hagoiim	huh-roh'shith-huh-goi'im
Harosheth-ha-goiim	huh-roh'shith-huh-goi'im
Harosheth-hagoyim	huh-roh'shith-huh-goi'im
Harosheth Hagoyim	huh-roh'shith-huh-goi'im
Harsa	hahr'suh
Harsha	hahr'shuh
Harsith	hahr'sith
Harum	hair'uhm
Harumaph	huh-r*oo*'maf
Haruphite	huh-r*oo*'f*i*t
Haruz	hair'uhz
Hasadiah	has'uh-d*i*'uh
Hasenuah	has'uh-n*oo*'uh
Hash	hash
Hashabiah	hash'uh-b*i*'uh
Hashabnah	huh-shab'nuh
Hashabneah	hash'uhb-nee'uh
Hashabneiah	hash'uhb-nee'yah
Hashabniah	hash'uhb-n*i*'uh
Hashbadana	hash-bad'uh-nuh
Hashbaddanah	hash-bad'uh-nuh
Hashem	hay'shim
Hashmonah	hash-moh'nuh
Hashub	hay'shuhb
Hashubah	huh-sh*oo*'buh
Hashum	hay'shuhm
Hashupha	huh-sh*oo*'fuh
Hasidaean	has'uh-dee'uhn

n **n**ot, ng si**ng**, o h**o**t, oh g**o**, oi b**oy**, oo f**oo**t, *oo* b**oo**t, oor p**oor**, or f**or**,
ou h**ow**, p **p**at, r **r**un, s **s**o, sh **s**ure, t **t**oe, th **th**in, *th* **th**en, ts **ts**etse,
tw **tw**in, uh **a**go, uhr h**er**, v **v**ow, w **w**eather, y **y**oung, z **z**one, zh vi**s**ion

61

Hasidean	has'uh-dee'uhn
Hasrah	haz'ruh
Hassenaah	has'uh-nay'uh
Hassenuah	has'uh-n*oo*'uh
Hasshub	hash'uhb
Hassophereth	ha-sof'uh-rith
Hasupha	huh-s*oo*'fuh
Hatach	hay'tak
Hathach	hay'thak
Hathath	hay'thath
Hatipha	huh-t*i*'fuh
Hatita	huh-t*i*'tuh
Hattaavah	huh-tay'uh-vah
Hatticon	hat'uh-kon
Hattil	hat'uhl
Hattush	hat'uhsh
Hauran	haw'ruhn
Havilah	hav'uh-luh
Havilah-by-shur	hav'uh-luh-b*i*-shuhr'
Havoth-Jair	hay'voth-jay'uhr
Havvothjair	hav'oth-jay'uhr
Havvoth-jair	hav'oth-jay'uhr
Havvoth Jair	hav'oth-jay'uhr
Hayamim	hay-yah'mim
Hazael	hay'zay-uhl
Hazaiah	huh-zay'yuh
Hazar	hay'zuhr
Hazaraddar	hay'zuhr-ad'uhr
Hazar-addar	hay'zuhr-ad'uhr
Hazar Addar	hay'zuhr-ad'uhr
Hazarenan	hay'zuhr-ee'nuhn
Hazar-enan	hay'zuhr-ee'nuhn
Hazar Enan	hay'zuhr-ee'nuhn
Hazarenon	hay'zuhr-ee'nuhn
Hazar-enon	hay'zuhr-ee'nuhn
Hazargaddah	hay'zuhr-gad'uh
Hazar-gaddah	hay'zuhr-gad'uh
Hazar Gaddah	hay'zuhr-gad'uh
Hazar-hatticon	hay'zuhr-hat'uh-kon
Hazar Hatticon	hay'zuhr-hat'uh-kon
Hazarmaveth	hay'zuhr-may'vith
Hazar-maveth	hay'zuhr-may'vith
Hazarshual	hay'zuhr-sh*oo*'uhl
Hazar-shual	hay'zuhr-sh*oo*'uhl
Hazar Shual	hay'zuhr-sh*oo*'uhl

---

a cat, ah father, ahr lard, air care, aw jaw, ay pay, b bug, ch chew, d do,
e, eh pet, ee seem, er error, f fun, g good, h hot, hw whether, i it, *i* sky,
ihr ear, j joke, k king, kh ch as in German *Buch*, ks vex, kw quill, l love, m mat,

Hazarsusah	hay′zuhr-*soo*′suh
Hazar-susah	hay′zuhr-*soo*′suh
Hazar Susah	hay′zuhr-*soo*′suh
Hazarsusim	hay′zuhr-*soo*′sim
Hazar-susim	hay′zuhr-*soo*′sim
Hazar Susim	hay′zuhr-*soo*′sim
Hazazon	haz′uh-zon
Hazazontamar	haz′uh-zon-tay′muhr
Hazazon-tamar	haz′uh-zon-tay′muhr
Hazazon Tamar	haz′uh-zon-tay′muhr
Hazelelponi	haz′uh-lel-poh′n*i*
Hazerhatticon	hay′zuhr-hat′uh-kon
Hazer-hatticon	hay′zuhr-hat′uh-kon
Hazer Hatticon	hay′zuhr-hat′uh-kon
Hazerim	huh-zihr′im
Hazeroth	huh-zihr′oth
Hazezon-tamar	haz′uh-zon-tay′muhr
Hazezon Tamar	haz′uh-zon-tay′muhr
Haziel	hay′zee-uhl
Hazo	hay′zoh
Hazor	hay′zor
Hazorhadattah	hay′zor-huh-dat′uh
Hazor-hadattah	hay′zor-huh-dat′uh
Hazor Hadattah	hay′zor-huh-dat′uh
Hazzebaim	haz′uh-bay′im
Hazzelelponi	haz′uh-lel-poh′n*i*
Hazzobebah	haz′oh-bee′buh
Hazzurim	haz′uh-rim
he	hay
Heber	hee′buhr
Heberite	hee′buh-r*i*t
Hebrew	hee′br*oo*
Hebrewess	hee′br*oo*-es
Hebron	hee′bruhn
Hebronite	hee′bruh-n*i*t
Hegai	heg′*i*
Hege	hee′gee
Hegemonides	hej′uh-moh′nuh-deez
Heglam	heg′luhm
Helah	hee′luh
Helam	hee′luhm
Helbah	hel′buh
Helbon	hel′bon
Helchiah	hel-k*i*′uh
Heldai	hel′d*i*

---

n **n**ot, ng si**ng**, o h**o**t, oh g**o**, oi b**oy**, oo f**oo**t, *oo* b**oo**t, oor p**oor**, or f**or**,
ou h**ow**, p **p**at, r **r**un, s **s**o, sh **s**ure, t **t**oe, th **th**in, *th* **th**en, ts **ts**etse,
tw **tw**in, uh **a**go, uhr h**er**, v **v**ow, w **w**eather, y **y**oung, z **z**one, zh vi**s**ion

63

Heleb	hee'lib
Helech	hee'lik
Heled	hee'lid
Helek	hee'lik
Helekite	hee'luh-k*i*t
Helem	hee'lim
Heleph	hee'lif
Heler	hee'luhr
Helez	hee'liz
Heli	hee'l*i*
Helias	hee'lee-uhs
Heliodorus	hee'lee-uh-dor'uhs
Heliopolis	hee'lee-op'uh-lis
Helkai	hel'k*i*
Helkath	hel'kath
Helkathhazzurim	hel'kath-haz'yoo-rim
Helkath-hazzurim	hel'kath-haz'yoo-rim
Helkath Hazzurim	hel'kath-haz'yoo-rim
Helkias	hel-k*i*'uhs
Hellenism	hel'uh-niz'uhm
Hellenist	hel'uh-nist
Hellenistic	hel'uh-nis'tik
Hellenization	hel'uh-n*i*-zay'shuhn
Hellez	hel'iz
Helon	hee'lon
Helper	help'uhr
Hemam	hee'mam
Heman	hee'muhn
Hemath	hee'math
Hemdan	hem'dan
Hen	hen
Hena	hen'uh
Henadad	hen'uh-dad
Henoch	hee'nuhk
Hepher	hee'fuhr
Hepherite	hee'fuh-r*i*t
Hephzibah	hef'zi-buh
Hephzi-bah	hef'zi-buh
Heradonijah	huhr-ad'uh-n*i*'juh
Hercules	huhr'kyuh-leez'
Heres	hihr'iz
Heresh	hihr'ish
Hereth	hihr'ith
Hermas	huhr'muhs
Hermes	huhr'meez

---

a cat, ah father, ahr lard, air care, aw jaw, ay pay, b bug, ch chew, d do,
e, eh pet, ee seem, er error, f fun, g good, h hot, hw whether, i it, *i* sky,
ihr ear, j joke, k king, kh ch as in German Buch, ks vex, kw quill, l love, m mat,

Hermogenes	huhr-moj′uh-neez
Hermon	huhr′muhn
Hermonite	huhr′muh-n*i*t
Herod	her′uhd
Herodian	hi-roh′dee-uhn
Herodias	hi-roh′dee-uhs
Herodion	hi-roh′dee-uhn
Hesed	hee′sid
Heshbon	hesh′bon
Heshbonite	hesh′buh-n*i*t
Heshmon	hesh′mon
Hesli	hes′l*i*
Heth	heth
heth	hayth
Hethlon	heth′lon
Hezeki	hez′uh-k*i*
Hezekiah	hez′uh-k*i*′uh
Hezion	hee′zee-uhn
Hezir	hee′zuhr
Hezrai	hez′r*i*
Hezro	hez′roh
Hezron	hez′ruhn
Hezronite	hez′ruh-n*i*t
Hiddai	hid′*i*
Hiddekel	hid′uh-kel
Hiel	h*i*′uhl
Hierapolis	h*i*′uh-rap′uh-lis
Hiereel	h*i*-ihr′ee-uhl
Hieremoth	h*i*-ihr′uh-moth
Hierielus	h*i*-ihr′i-ee′luhs
Hiermas	h*i*-uhr′muhs
Hieronymus	h*i*′uh-ron′uh-muhs
Higgaion	hi-gay′yon
Hilen	h*i*′luhn
Hilkath	hil′kath
Hilkiah	hil-k*i*′uh
Hillel	hil′uhl
hin	hin
Hinnom	hin′uhm
hippodrome	hip′uh-drohm′
Hirah	h*i*′ruh
Hiram	h*i*′ruhm
Hircanus	hihr-kay′nuhs
Hittite	hit′t*i*t
Hivite	hiv′*i*t

n **not**, ng **sing**, o **hot**, oh **go**, oi **boy**, oo **foot**, *oo* **boot**, oor **poor**, or **for**,
ou **how**, p **pat**, r **run**, s **so**, sh **sure**, t **toe**, th **thin**, *th* **then**, ts **tsetse**,
tw **twin**, uh **ago**, uhr **her**, v **vow**, w **weather**, y **young**, z **zone**, zh **vision**

Hizki	hiz′k*i*
Hizkiah	hiz-k*i*′uh
Hizkijah	hiz-k*i*′juh
Hobab	hoh′bab
Hobah	hoh′buh
Hobaiah	hoh-bay′yuh
Hod	hod
Hodaiah	hoh-day′yuh
Hodaviah	hod′uh-v*i*′uh
Hodesh	hoh′desh
Hodevah	hoh-dee′vuh
Hodiah	hoh-d*i*′uh
Hodijah	hoh-d*i*′juh
Hodshi	hod′sh*i*
Hoglah	hog′luh
Hoham	hoh′ham
Holofernes	hol′uh-fuhr′neez
Holon	hoh′lon
Holy Ghost	hoh′lee-gohst′
Holy Spirit	hoh′lee-spihr′it
Homam	hoh′mam
homer	hoh′muhr
hoopoe	h*oo*′p*oo*
Hophni	hof′n*i*
Hophra	hof′ruh
Hor	hor
Horam	hor′am
Horeb	hor′eb
Horem	hor′em
Horesh	hor′esh
Horhaggidgad	hor′huh-gid′gad
Hor-haggidgad	hor′huh-gid′gad
Hor Haggidgad	hor′huh-gid′gad
Hor-hagidgad	hor′huh-gid′gad
Hor Hagidgad	hor′huh-gid′gad
Hori	hor′*i*
Horim	hor′im
Horite	hor′*i*t
Hormah	hor′muh
Horon	hor′on
Horonaim	hor′uh-nay′im
Horonite	hor′uh-n*i*t
Hosah	hoh′suh
hosanna	hoh-zan′uh
Hosea	hoh-zay′uh

a cat, ah father, ahr lard, air care, aw jaw, ay pay, b bug, ch chew, d do,
e, eh pet, ee seem, er error, f fun, g good, h hot, hw whether, i it, *i* sky,
ihr ear, j joke, k king, kh ch as in German *Buch*, ks vex, kw quill, l love, m mat,

Hoshaiah	hoh-shay'yuh
Hoshama	hosh'uh-muh
Hoshea	hoh-shee'uh
Hotham	hoh'thuhm
Hothan	hoh'thuhn
Hothir	hoh'thuhr
Hozai	hoh'z*i*
Hozeh	hoh'zeh
Hubbah	huh'buh
Huddai	huh'd*i*
Hukkok	huh'kok
Hukok	hy*oo*'kok
Hul	huhl
Huldah	huhl'duh
Humtah	huhm'tuh
Hupham	hy*oo*'fuhm
Huphamite	hy*oo*'fuh-m*i*t
Huppah	hup'uh
Huppim	hup'im
Huppite	hup'*i*t
Hur	huhr
Hurai	hyoor'*i*
Huram	hyoor'uhm
Huramabi	hyoor'uhm-ay'b*i*
Huram-abi	hyoor'uhm-ay'b*i*
Huri	hyoor'*i*
Hus	huhs
Husha	hoosh'uh
Hushah	hoosh'uh
Hushai	hoosh'*i*
Husham	hoosh'uhm
Hushathite	hoosh'uh-th*i*t
Hushim	hoosh'im
Hushite	hoosh'*i*t
Huz	huhz
Huzoth	huh'zoth
Huzzab	huh'zuhb
Hydaspes	h*i*-das'peez
Hymenaeus	h*i*'muh-nee'uhs
Hymeneus	h*i*'muh-nee'uhs
Hyrcanus	hihr-kay'nuhs
hyssop	his'uhp

---

n not, ng sing, o hot, oh go, oi boy, oo foot, *oo* boot, oor poor, or for,
ou how, p pat, r run, s so, sh sure, t toe, th thin, *th* then, ts tsetse,
tw twin, uh ago, uhr her, v vow, w weather, y young, z zone, zh vision

I

Ibhar	ib'hahr
Ibleam	ib'lee-uhm
Ibneiah	ib-nee'yah
Ibnijah	ib-n*i*'juh
Ibri	ib'r*i*
Ibsam	ib'sam
Ibzan	ib'zan
Ichabod	ik'uh-bod
I-chabod	i'kuh-bod
Iconium	*i*-koh'nee-uhm
Idalah	id'uh-luh
Idbash	id'bash
Iddo	id'oh
Iduel	id'y*oo*-uhl
Idumaea	id'y*oo*-mee'uh
Idumaean	id'y*oo*-mee'uhn
Idumea	id'y*oo*-mee'uh
Idumean	id'y*oo*-mee'uhn
Iezer	*i*-ee'zuhr
Iezerite	*i*-ee'zuh-r*i*t
Igal	*i*'gal
Igdaliah	ig'duh-l*i*'uh
Igeal	*i*'gee-uhl
Iim	*i*'im
Iishvah	*i*-ish'vuh
Ije-abarim	*i*'juh-ab'uh-rim
Ije Abarim	*i*'juh-ab'uh-rim
Ijim	*i*'jim
Ijon	*i*'jon
Ikkesh	ik'ish
Ilai	*i*'l*i*
Iliadun	i-l*i*'uh-duhn
Illyria	i-lihr'ee-uh
Illyricum	i-lihr'i-kuhm
Imalkue	i-mal'ky*oo*-ee
Imla	im'luh
Imlah	im'luh
Immanuel	i-man'y*oo*-uhl
Immer	im'uhr
Immite	im'*i*t
Imna	im'nuh
Imnah	im'nuh

---

a cat, ah father, ahr lard, air care, aw jaw, ay pay, b bug, ch chew, d do,
e, eh pet, ee seem, er error, f fun, g good, h hot, hw whether, i it, *i* sky,
ihr ear, j joke, k king, kh ch as in German *Buch*, ks vex, kw quill, l love, m mat,

Imnite	im′n*i*t
Imrah	im′ruh
Imri	im′r*i*
India	in′dee-uh
Indian	in′dee-uhn
Iob	*i*′ohb
Ionian	*i*-oh′nee-uhn
iota	*i*-oh′tuh
Iphdeiah	if-dee′yah
Iphedeiah	if′uh-dee′yah
Iphtah	if′tuh
Iphtahel	if′tuh-el′
Iphtah-el	if′tuh-el′
Iphtah El	if′tuh-el′
Ir	ihr
Ira	*i*′ruh
Irad	*i*′rad
Iram	*i*′ram
Ir-hamelah	ihr-ham′uh-luh
Iri	*i*′r*i*
Irijah	*i*-r*i*′juh
Ir-Moab	ihr-moh′ab
Irnahash	ihr-nay′hash
Ir-nahash	ihr-nay′hash
Ir Nahash	ihr-nay′hash
Iron	*i*′ron
Irpeel	ihr′pee-uhl
Irshemesh	ihr-shem′ish
Ir-shemesh	ihr-shem′ish
Ir Shemesh	ihr-shem′ish
Iru	*i*′r*oo*
Isaac	*i*′zik
Isai	*i*′z*i*
Isaiah	*i*-zay′yuh
Isaias	*i*′zay′yuhs
Iscah	is′kuh
Iscariot	is-kair′ee-uht
Isdael	iz′dee-uhl
Ish	ish
Ishbaal	ish′bay-uhl
Ishbah	ish′buh
Ishbak	ish′bak
Ishbibenob	ish′b*i*-bee′nob
Ishbi-benob	ish′b*i*-bee′nob
Ishbosheth	ish-boh′shith

---

n **n**ot, ng si**ng**, o h**o**t, oh g**o**, oi b**oy**, oo f**oo**t, *oo* b**oo**t, oor p**oor**, or f**or**,
ou h**ow**, p **p**at, r **r**un, s **s**o, sh **s**ure, t **t**oe, th **th**in, *th* **th**en, ts **ts**etse,
tw **tw**in, uh **ago**, uhr h**er**, v **v**ow, w **w**eather, y **y**oung, z **z**one, zh vi**s**ion

Ish-bosheth	ish-boh'shith
Ish-hai	ish'h*i*
Ishhod	ish'hod
Ishi	ish'*i*
Ishiah	i-sh*i*'uh
Ishijah	i-sh*i*'juh
Ishma	ish'muh
Ishmael	ish'may-uhl
Ishmaelite	ish'may-uh-l*i*t
Ishmaiah	ish-may'yuh
Ishmeelite	ish'mee-uh-l*i*t
Ishmerai	ish'muh-r*i*
Ishod	ish'od
Ishpah	ish'puh
Ishpan	ish'pan
Ish-tob	ish'tob
Ishuah	ish'y*oo*-uh
Ishuai	ish'y*oo*-*i*
Ishui	ish'y*oo*-*i*
Ishvah	ish'vuh
Ishvi	ish'v*i*
Ishvite	ish'v*i*t
Ismachiah	is'muh-k*i*'uh
Ismael	is'may-uhl
Ismaiah	is-may'yuh
Ismakiah	is'muh-k*i*'uh
Ispa	is'puh
Ispah	is'puh
Israel	iz'ray-uhl
Israelite	iz'ray-uh-l*i*t
Israelitish	iz'ray-uh-l*i*t'ish
Issachar	is'uh-kahr'
Issacharite	is'uh-kuh-r*i*t
Isshiah	i-sh*i*'uh
Isshijah	i-sh*i*'juh
Istalcurus	is'tuhl-kyoor'uhs
Isuah	is'y*oo*-uh
Isui	is'y*oo*-*i*
Italian	i-tal'yuhn
Italica	i-tal'i-kuh
Italy	it'uh-lee
Ithai	ith'*i*
Ithamar	ith'uh-mahr
Ithiel	ith'ee-uhl
Ithlah	ith'luh

---

a cat, ah father, ahr lard, air care, aw jaw, ay pay, b bug, ch chew, d do,
e, eh pet, ee seem, er error, f fun, g good, h hot, hw whether, i it, *i* sky,
ihr ear, j joke, k king, kh ch as in German Buch, ks vex, kw quill, l love, m mat,

Ithmah	ith'muh
Ithnan	ith'nan
Ithra	ith'ruh
Ithran	ith'ran
Ithream	ith'ree-uhm
Ithrite	ith'r*i*t
Ittah-kazin	it'uh-kay'zin
Ittai	it'*i*
Ituraea	it'yoor-ee'uh
Iturea	it'yoor-ee'uh
Ivah	*i*'vuh
Ivvah	iv'uh
Iyeabarim	*i*'yuh-ab'uh-rim
Iye-abarim	*i*'yuh-ab'uh-rim
Iye Abarim	*i*'yuh-ab'uh-rim
Iyim	*i*'yim
Iyyob	*i*'yohb
Izar	*i*'zahr
Izarahiah	iz'uh-ruh-h*i*'uh
Izehar	iz'uh-hahr
Izeharite	iz'uh-hah-r*i*t
Izhar	iz'hahr
Izharite	iz'huh-r*i*t
Izliah	iz-l*i*'uh
Izrahiah	iz'ruh-h*i*'uh
Izrahite	iz'ruh-h*i*t
Izri	iz'r*i*
Izziah	i-z*i*'uh

J

Jaakan	jay'uh-kan
Jaakanite	jay-a'kuh-n*i*t
Jaakobah	jay-uh-koh'buh
Jaakobath	jay-uh-koh'bath
Jaala	jay'uh-luh
Jaalah	jay'uh-luh
Jaalam	jay'uh-lam
Jaan	jay'an
Jaanai	jay'uh-n*i*
Jaar	jay'uhr

---

n **n**ot, ng si**ng**, o h**o**t, oh g**o**, oi b**o**y, oo f**oo**t, *oo* b**oo**t, oor p**oo**r, or f**or**,
ou h**ow**, p **p**at, r **r**un, s **s**o, sh **s**ure, t **t**oe, th **th**in, *th* **th**en, ts **ts**etse,
tw **tw**in, uh **a**go, uhr h**er**, v **v**ow, w **w**eather, y **y**oung, z **z**one, zh vi**s**ion

Jaareoregim	jay'uh-ree-or'uh-gim
Jaare-Oregim	jay'uh-ree-or'uh-gim
Jaareshiah	jay'uh-ree-shi'uh
Jaasai	jay'uh-si
Jaasau	jay'uh-saw
Jaasiel	jay-ay'see-uhl
Jaasu	jay'uh-soo
Jaazaniah	jay-az'uh-ni'uh
Jaazer	jay'uh-zuhr
Jaaziah	jay'uh-zi'uh
Jaaziel	jay-ay'zee-uhl
Jabal	jay'buhl
Jabbok	jab'uhk
Jabesh	jay'bish
Jabeshgilead	jay'bish-gil'ee-uhd
Jabesh-gilead	jay'bish-gil'ee-uhd
Jabesh Gilead	jay'bish-gil'ee-uhd
Jabez	jay'biz
Jabin	jay'bin
Jabneel	jab'nee-uhl
Jabneh	jab'neh
Jacan	jay'kuhn
Jachan	jay'kuhn
Jachin	jay'kin
Jachinite	jay'kuh-nit
jacinth	jay'sinth
Jacob	jay'kuhb
Jacubus	juh-kyoo'buhs
Jada	jay'duh
Jadah	jay'duh
Jadau	jay'daw
Jaddai	jad'i
Jaddua	jad'yoo-uh
Jaddus	jad'uhs
Jadon	jay'don
Jael	jay'uhl
Jagur	jay'guhr
Jah	jah
Jahaleleel	jay'huh-lel'ee-uhl
Jahath	jay'hath
Jahaz	jay'haz
Jahaza	juh-hay'zuh
Jahazah	juh-hay'zuh
Jahaziah	jay'huh-zi'uh
Jahaziel	juh-hay'zee-uhl

---

a cat, ah father, ahr lard, air care, aw jaw, ay pay, b bug, ch chew, d do,
e, eh pet, ee seem, er error, f fun, g good, h hot, hw whether, i it, *i* sky,
ihr ear, j joke, k king, kh ch as in German *Buch*, ks vex, kw quill, l love, m mat,

Jahdai	jah'd*i*
Jahdiel	jah'dee-uhl
Jahdo	jah'doh
Jahel	jay'huhl
Jahleel	jah'lee-uhl
Jahleelite	jah'lee-uh-l*i*t
Jahmai	jah'm*i*
Jahzah	jah'zuh
Jahzeel	jah'zee-uhl
Jahzeelite	jah'zee-uh-l*i*t
Jahzeiah	jah-zee'yah
Jahzerah	jah'zuh-ruh
Jahziel	jah'zee-uhl
Jair	jay'uhr
Jairite	jay'uh-r*i*t
Jairus	jay-*i*'ruhs
Jakan	jay'kuhn
Jakeh	jay'kuh
Jakim	jay'kim
Jakin	jay'kin
Jakinite	jay'kuh-n*i*t
Jalam	jay'luhm
Jalon	jay'lon
Jambres	jam'briz
Jambri	jam'br*i*
James	jaymz
Jamin	jay'min
Jaminite	jay'mi-n*i*t
Jamlech	jam'lik
Jamnia	jam'nee-uh
Jamnian	jam'nee-uhn
Janai	jay'n*i*
Janim	jay'nim
Janna	jan'uh
Jannai	jan'*i*
Jannes	jan'iz
Janoah	juh-noh'uh
Janohah	juh-noh'huh
Janum	jay'nuhm
Japheth	jay'fith
Japhia	juh-f*i*'uh
Japhlet	jaf'lit
Japhleti	jaf'luh-t*i*
Japhletite	jaf'luh-t*i*t
Japho	jay'foh

n **not**, ng **sing**, o **hot**, oh **go**, oi **boy**, oo **foot**, *oo* **boot**, oor **poor**, or **for**,
ou **how**, p **pat**, r **run**, s **so**, sh **sure**, t **toe**, th **thin**, *th* **then**, ts **tsetse**,
tw **twin**, uh **ago**, uhr **her**, v **vow**, w **weather**, y **young**, z **zone**, zh **vision**

Jarah	jair'uh
Jareb	jair'ib
Jared	jair'id
Jaresiah	jair'uh-si'uh
Jarha	jahr'huh
Jarib	jair'ib
Jarimoth	jair'uh-moth
Jarkon	jahr'kon
Jarmuth	jahr'muhth
Jaroah	juh-roh'uh
Jasael	jay'say-uhl
Jashar	jay'shuhr
Jashen	jay'shuhn
Jasher	jay'shuhr
Jashobeam	juh-shoh'bee-uhm
Jashub	jay'shuhb
Jashubi-lehem	juh-shoo'buh-lee'hem
Jashubi Lehem	juh-shoo'buh-lee'hem
Jashubite	jay'shuh-bit
Jasiel	jay'see-uhl
Jason	jay'suhn
Jasubus	juh-soo'buhs
Jatal	jay'tuhl
Jathan	jay'thuhn
Jathniel	jath'nee-uhl
Jattir	jat'uhr
Javan	jay'vuhn
Jazer	jay'zuhr
Jaziz	jay'ziz
Jearim	jee'uh-rim
Jeaterai	jee-at'uh-ri
Jeatherai	jee-ath'uh-ri
Jeberechiah	ji-ber'uh-ki'uh
Jeberekiah	ji-ber'uh-ki'uh
Jebus	jee'buhs
Jebusi	jeb'yoo-si
Jebusite	jeb'yoo-sit
Jecamiah	jek'uh-mi'uh
Jechiliah	jek'uh-li'uh
Jecholiah	jek'uh-li'uh
Jechoniah	jek'uh-ni'uh
Jechonias	jek'uh-ni'uhs
Jecoliah	jek'uh-li'uh
Jeconiah	jek'uh-ni'uh
Jeconias	jek'uh-ni-uhs

a cat, ah father, ahr lard, air care, aw jaw, ay pay, b bug, ch chew, d do,
e, eh pet, ee seem, er error, f fun, g good, h hot, hw whether, i it, i sky,
ihr ear, j joke, k king, kh ch as in German Buch, ks vex, kw quill, l love, m mat,

Jedaiah	ji-day'-yuh
Jeddu	jed'*oo*
Jedeus	jed'ee-uhs
Jediael	ji-d*i*'ay-uhl
Jedidah	ji-d*i*'duh
Jedidiah	jed'uh-d*i*'uh
Jeduthun	ji-dy*oo*'thuhn
Jeeli	jee'uh-l*i*
Jeelus	ji-ee'luhs
Jeezer	ji-ee'zuhr
Jeezerite	ji-ee'zuh-r*i*t
Jegarsahadutha	jee'guhr-say-huh-d*oo*'thuh
Jegar-sahadutha	jee'guhr-say-huh-d*oo*'thuh
Jegar Sahadutha	jee'guhr-say-huh-d*oo*'-thuh
Jehaleleel	jee'huh-lee'lee-uhl
Jehalelel	ji-hal'uh-luhl
Jehallel	juh-hal'uhl
Jehallelel	ji-hal'uh-luhl
Jehath	jee'hath
Jehaziel	ji-haz'ee-uhl
Jehdeiah	ji-dee'yah
Jehezekel	ji-hez'uh-kel
Jehezkel	ji-hez'kel
Jehiah	ji-h*i*'uh
Jehiel	ji-h*i*'uhl
Jehieli	ji-h*i*'uh-l*i*
Jehielite	ji-h*i*'uh-l*i*t
Jehizkiah	jee'hiz-k*i*'uh
Jehoadah	ji-hoh'uh-duh
Jehoaddah	ji-hoh'uh-duh
Jehoaddan	ji-hoh'uh-duhn
Jehoaddin	ji-hoh'uh-din
Jehoahaz	ji-hoh'uh-haz
Jehoash	ji-hoh'ash
Jehohanan	jee'hoh-hay'nuhn
Jehoiachin	ji-hoi'uh-kin
Jehoiada	ji-hoi'uh-duh
Jehoiakim	ji-hoi'uh-kim
Jehoiarib	ji-hoi'uh-rib
Jehonadab	ji-hoh'nuh-dab
Jehonathan	ji-hon'uh-thuhn
Jehoram	ji-hor'uhm
Jehoshabeath	jee'hoh-shab'ee-ath
Jehoshaphat	ji-hosh'uh-fat
Jehosheba	ji-hosh'uh-buh

---

n not, ng sing, o hot, oh go, oi boy, oo foot, *oo* boot, oor poor, or for,
ou how, p pat, r run, s so, sh sure, t toe, th thin, *th* then, ts tsetse,
tw twin, uh ago, uhr her, v vow, w weather, y young, z zone, zh vision

Jehoshua	ji-hosh'yoo-uh
Jehoshuah	ji-hosh'yoo-uh
Jehovah	ji-hoh'vuh
Jehovah-jireh	ji-hoh'vuh-ji'ruh
Jehovah-nissi	ji-hoh'vuh-nis'i
Jehovah-shalom	ji-hoh'vuh-shah'lohm
Jehozabad	ji-hoh'zuh-bad
Jehozadak	ji-hoh'zuh-dak
Jehu	jee'hyoo
Jehubbah	ji-hub'uh
Jehucal	ji-hyoo'kuhl
Jehud	jee'huhd
Jehudi	ji-hyoo'di
Jehudijah	jee'huh-di'juh
Jehuel	ji-hyoo'uhl
Jehus	jee'huhs
Jehush	jee'huhsh
Jeiel	ji-i'uhl
Jekabzeel	ji-kab'zee-uhl
Jekameam	jek'uh-mee'uhm
Jekamiah	jek'uh-mi'uh
Jekuthiel	ji-kyoo'thee-uhl
Jemima	ji-mi'muh
Jemimah	ji-mi'muh
Jeminah	ji-mi'nuh
Jemnaan	jem'nay-uhn
Jemuel	jem'yoo-uhl
Jenual	jen'yoo-uhl
Jephte	jef'tee
Jephthae	jef'thee
Jephthah	jef'thuh
Jephunneh	ji-fuhn'uh
Jerah	jihr'uh
Jerahmeel	ji-rah'mee-uhl
Jerahmeelite	ji-rah'mee-uh-lit
Jerechus	jer'uh-kuhs
Jered	jihr'id
Jeremai	jer'uh-mi
Jeremiah	jer'uh-mi'uh
Jeremias	jer'uh-mi'uhs
Jeremiel	ji-rem'ee-uhl
Jeremoth	jer'uh-moth
Jeremy	jer'uh-mee
Jeriah	ji-ri'uh
Jeribai	jer'uh-bi

a cat, ah father, ahr lard, air care, aw jaw, ay pay, b bug, ch chew, d do,
e, eh pet, ee seem, er error, f fun, g good, h hot, hw whether, i it, i sky,
ihr ear, j joke, k king, kh ch as in German Buch, ks vex, kw quill, l love, m mat,

Jericho	jer'uh-koh
Jeriel	jihr'*i*-uhl
Jerijah	ji-r*i*'jah
Jerimoth	jer'i-moth
Jerioth	jer'ee-oth
Jeroboam	jer'uh-boh'uhm
Jeroham	ji-roh'ham
Jerubbaal	ji'ruhb-bay'uhl
Jerub-baal	ji'ruhb-bay'uhl
Jerubbesheth	ji-rub'uh-sheth
Jerub-besheth	ji-rub'uh-sheth
Jeruel	ji-r*oo*'uhl
Jerusa	ji-r*oo*'suh
Jerusah	ji-r*oo*'suh
Jerusalem	ji-r*oo*'suh-luhm
Jerusha	ji-r*oo*'shah
Jerushah	ji-r*oo*'shah
Jesaiah	ji-say'yuh
Jesarelah	jes'uh-ree'luh
Jeshaiah	ji-shay'yuh
Jeshanah	jesh'uh-nuh
Jesharelah	jesh'uh-ree'luh
Jeshebeab	ji-sheb'ee-ab
Jesher	jesh'uhr
Jeshimon	ji-sh*i*'mon
Jeshimoth	ji-sh*i*'moth
Jeshishai	ji-shish'*i*
Jeshohaiah	jesh'uh-hay'yah
Jeshoshaphat	ji-shosh'uh-fat
Jeshua	jesh'y*oo*-uh
Jeshuah	jesh'y*oo*-uh
Jeshurun	jesh'uh-ruhn
Jeshush	jesh'ush
Jesiah	ji-s*i*'uh
Jesimiel	ji-sim'ee-uhl
Jesimoth	ji-s*i*'moth
Jesse	jes'ee
Jesshiah	ji-sh*i*'uh
Jessue	jesh'y*oo*-ee
Jesu	je's*oo*
Jesui	jes'y*oo*-i
Jesuite	jes'y*oo*-it
Jesurun	jes'uh-ruhn
Jesus	jee'zuhs
Jesus ben-sira	jee'zuhs-ben-s*i*'ruh

n not, ng sing, o hot, oh go, oi boy, oo foot, *oo* boot, oor poor, or for,
ou how, p pat, r run, s so, sh sure, t toe, th thin, *th* then, ts tsetse,
tw twin, uh ago, uhr her, v vow, w weather, y young, z zone, zh vision

Jesus ben-Sirach	jee'zuhs-ben-si'ruhk
Jether	jee'thuhr
Jetherai	jeth'uh-ri
Jetheth	jee'theth
Jethlah	jeth'luh
Jethro	jeth'roh
Jetta	jet'uh
Jetur	jee'tuhr
Jeuel	ji-yoo'uhl
Jeush	jee'ush
Jeuz	jee'uhz
Jew	joo
Jewess	joo'es
Jewish	joo'ish
Jewry	joo'ree
Jezaniah	jez'uh-ni'uh
Jezebel	jez'uh-bel
Jezelus	jez'uh-luhs
Jezer	jee'zuhr
Jezerite	jee'zuh-rit
Jeziah	ji-zi'uh
Jeziel	jee'zee-uhl
Jezliah	jez-li'uh
Jezoar	ji-zoh'ahr
Jezrahel	jez'ruh-hel
Jezrahiah	jez'ruh-hi'uh
Jezreel	jez'ree-uhl
Jezreelite	jez'ree-uh-lit
Jezreelitess	jez'ree-uh-lit-es
Jibsam	jib'sam
Jidlaph	jid'laf
Jimna	jim'nuh
Jimnah	jim'nuh
Jimnite	jim'nit
Jiphtah	jif'tuh
Jiphthah-el	jif'thuh-el
Jipithah El	jif'thuh-el
Jiptah	jip'tuh
Jishui	jish'yoo-ee
Jisshiah	ji-shi'uh
Jithra	jith'ruh
Jithran	jith'ruhn
Jizliah	jiz-li'uh
Jizri	jiz'ri
Joab	joh'ab

---

a cat, ah father, ahr lard, air care, aw jaw, ay pay, b bug, ch chew, d do,
e, eh pet, ee seem, er error, f fun, g good, h hot, hw whether, i it, i sky,
ihr ear, j joke, k king, kh ch as in German Buch, ks vex, kw quill, l love, m mat,

Joachaz	joh'uh-kaz
Joachim	joh'uh-kim
Joacim	joh'uh-kim
Joadanus	joh-ad'uh-nuhs
Joah	joh'uh
Joahaz	joh'uh-haz
Joakim	joh'uh-kim
Joanan	joh-ay'nuhn
Joanna	joh-an'uh
Joannan	joh-an'uhn
Joannas	joh-an'uhs
Joarib	joh'uh-rib
Joash	joh'ash
Joatham	joh'uh-thuhm
Joazabdus	joh'uh-zab'duhs
Job	johb
Jobab	joh'bab
Jochanan	joh'kuh-nuhn
Jochebed	jok'uh-bed
jod	johd
Joda	joh'duh
Jodan	joh'duhn
Joed	joh'ed
Joel	joh'uhl
Joelah	joh-ee'luh
Joezer	joh-ee'zuhr
Jogbehah	jog'buh-hah
Jogli	jog'li
Joha	joh'huh
Johanan	joh-hay'nuhn
Johannan	joh-han'uhn
Johannes	joh-han'iz
John	jon
John-Mark	jon-mahrk'
Johojanan	joh'hoh-jay'nuhn
Joiada	joi'uh-duh
Joiakim	joi'uh-kim
Joiarib	joi'uh-rib
Jokdeam	jok'dee-uhm
Jokim	joh'kim
Jokmeam	jok'mee-uhm
Jokneam	jok'nee-uhm
Jokshan	jok'shan
Joktan	jok'tan
Joktheel	jok'thee-uhl

n **n**ot, ng si**ng**, o h**o**t, oh g**o**, oi b**oy**, oo f**oo**t, *oo* b**oo**t, oor p**oor**, or f**or**,
ou h**ow**, p **p**at, r **r**un, s **s**o, sh **s**ure, t **t**oe, th **th**in, *th* **th**en, ts **ts**etse,
tw **tw**in, uh **a**go, uhr h**er**, v **v**ow, w **w**eather, y **y**oung, z **z**one, zh vi**s**ion

Jona	joh′nuh
Jonadab	joh′nuh-dab
Jonah	joh′nuh
Jonam	joh′nuhm
Jonan	joh′nuhn
Jonas	joh′nuhs
Jonathan	jon′uh-thuhn
Jonathas	jon′uh-thuhs
Jonath-elem-rechokim	joh′nuth-ee′luhm-ri-koh′kim
Jonath Elem Rehoqim	joh′nuth-ee′luhm-ri-hoh′kim
Joppa	jop′uh
Jorah	jor′*i*
Jorai	jor′*i*
Joram	jor′uhm
Jordan	jor′duhn
Joribas	juh-r*i*′buhs
Joribus	juh-r*i*′buhs
Jorim	jor′im
Jorkeam	jor′kee-uhm
Jorkoam	jor′koh-uhm
Josabad	joh′suh-bad
Josaphat	jos′uh-fat
Josaphias	joh′soh-f*i*′uhs
Jose	joh′see
Josech	joh′sik
Josedec	joh′suh-dek
Josedech	joh′suh-dek
Joseph	joh′sif
Josephite	joh′suh-f*i*t
Josephus	joh-see′fuhs
Joses	joh′siz
Joshah	joh′shuh
Joshaphat	josh′uh-fat
Joshaviah	josh′uh-v*i*′uh
Joshbekashah	josh′bi-kay′shuh
Josheb	joh′shib
Joshebbasshebeth	joh′shib-buh-shee′bith
Josheb-basshebeth	joh′shib-buh-shee′bith
Joshibiah	josh′uh-b*i*′uh
Joshua	josh′y*oo*-uh
Josiah	joh-s*i*′uh
Josias	joh-s*i*′uhs
Josibiah	jos-i-b*i*′uh
Josiphiah	jos-i-f*i*′uh
Josue	jos-*oo*′ee

a cat, ah father, ahr lard, air care, aw jaw, ay pay, b bug, ch chew, d do,
e, eh pet, ee seem, er error, f fun, g good, h hot, hw whether, i it, *i* sky,
ihr ear, j joke, k king, kh ch as in German Buch, ks vex, kw quill, l love, m mat,

jot	jot
Jotbah	jot′buh
Jotbath	jot′bath
Jotbathah	jot′buh-thuh
Jotham	joh′thuhm
Jozabad	joh′zuh-bad
Jozacar	joh′zuh-kahr
Jozachar	joh′zuh-kahr
Jozadak	joh′zuh-dak
Jubal	joo′buhl
jubile	joo′buh-lee
jubilee	joo′buh-lee
;ucal	joo′kuhl
Juda	joo′duh
Judaea	joo-dee′uh
Judaean	joo-dee′uhn
Judah	joo′duh
Judahite	joo′duh-hit
Judaism	joo′duh-iz-uhm
Judas	joo′duhs
Judas-Iscariot	joo′duhs-is-kair′ee-uht
Judas Iscariot	joo′duhs-is-kair′ee-uht
Jude	jood
Judea	joo-dee′uh
Judean	joo-dee′uhn
Judges	juhj′iz
Judith	joo′dith
Juel	joo′uhl
Julia	joo′lee-uh
Julius	joo′lee-uhs
Junia	joo′nee-uh
Junias	joo′nee-uhs
Jupiter	joo′puh-tuhr
Jushabhesed	joo′shab-hee′sid
Jushab-hesed	joo′shab-hee′sid
Jushab Hesed	joo′shab-hee′sid
Justus	juhs′tuhs
Jutah	joo′tuh
Juttah	jut′uh

---

n **not**, ng **sing**, o **hot**, oh **go**, oi **boy**, oo **foot**, *oo* **boot**, oor **poor**, or **for**,
ou **how**, p **pat**, r **run**, s **so**, sh **sure**, t **toe**, th **thin**, *th* **then**, ts **tsetse**,
tw **twin**, uh **ago**, uhr **her**, v **vow**, w **weather**, y **young**, z **zone**, zh **vision**

K

kab	kab
Kabzeel	kab'zee-uhl
Kades	kay'deez
Kadesh	kay'dish
Kadeshbarnea	kay'dish-bahr'nee-uh
Kadesh-barnea	kay'dish-bahr'nee-uh
Kadesh Barnea	kay'dish-bahr'nee-uh
Kadesh-Meribah	kay'dish-mer'uh-buh
Kadish	kay'dish
Kadmiel	kad'mee-uhl
Kadmonite	kad'muh-n*i*t
Kain	kayn
Kaiwan	k*i*'wuhn
Kallai	kal'*i*
Kamon	kay'muhn
Kanah	kay'nuh
kaph	kaf
Kareah	kuh-ree'uh
Karim	kair'im
Karka	kahr'kuh
Karkaa	kahr'kay-uh
Karkor	kahr'kor
Karnaim	kahr-nay'im
Karnion	kahr'nee-uhn
Kartah	kahr'tuh
Kartan	kahr'tan
Kaserin	kas'uh-rin
Kattah	kat'uh
Kattath	kat'ath
Kebar	kee'bahr
Kedar	kee'duhr
Kedem	kee'duhm
Kedemah	ked'uh-muh
Kedemite	ked'uh-m*i*t
Kedemoth	ked'uh-moth
Kedesh	kee'dish
Kedesh-naphtali	kee'dish-naf'tuh-l*i*
Kedorlaomer	ked'or-lay'oh-muhr
Kedron	kee'druhn
Kehelathah	kee'huh-lay'thuh
Keilah	kee-*i*'luh
Kelaiah	ki-lay'yuh

---

a cat, ah father, ahr lard, air care, aw jaw, ay pay, b bug, ch chew, d do,
e, eh pet. ee seem, er error, f fun, g good, h hot, hw whether, i it, *i* sky,
ihr ear, j joke, k king, kh ch as in German *Buch*, ks vex, kw quill, l love, m mat,

Kelal	kee'lal
Kelita	ki-li'tuh
Kelub	kee'luhb
Keluhi	kel'yoo-hi
Kemuel	kem'yoo-uhl
Kenaanah	ki-nay'uh-nuh
Kenan	kee'nuhn
Kenani	ki-nay'ni
Kenaniah	ken'uh-ni'uh
Kenath	kee'nath
Kenaz	kee'naz
Kenez	kee'niz
Kenezite	ken'uh-zit
Kenezzite	ken'uh-zit
Kenite	ken'it
Kenizzite	ken'uh-zit
Kephar-ammoni	kee'fuhr-am'oh-ni
Kephar Ammoni	kee'fuhr-am'oh-ni
Kephirah	ki-fi'ruh
Keran	kee'ruhn
Kerenhappuch	ker'uhn-hap'uhk
Keren-happuch	ker'uhn-hap'uhk
Kerethite	ker'uh-thit
Kerioth	ker'ee-oth
Keriothhezron	ker'ee-oth-hez'ruhn
Kerioth-hezron	ker'ee-oth-hez'ruhn
Kerioth Hezron	ker'ee-oth-hez'ruhn
Kerith	kihr'ith
Keros	kihr'os
Kerub	kihr'uhb
Kesalon	kes'uh-luhn
Kesed	kee'sid
Kesil	kee'sil
Kesulloth	ki-suhl'oth
Ketab	kee'tab
Kethuvim	kuh-thoo'vim
Keturah	ki-tyoor'uh
Keveh	kee'vuh
Kezia	ki-zi'uh
Keziah	ki-zi'uh
Kezib	kee'zib
Keziz	kee'ziz
Kibrothhattaavah	kib'roth-huh-tay'uh-vuh
Kibroth-hattaavah	kib'roth-huh-tay'uh-vuh
Kibroth Hattaavah	kib'roth-huh-tay'uh-vuh

---

n **n**ot, ng si**ng**, o h**o**t, oh g**o**, oi b**oy**, oo f**oo**t, oo b**oo**t, oor p**oor**, or f**or**,
ou h**ow**, p **p**at, r **r**un, s **s**o, sh **s**ure, t **t**oe, th **th**in, th **th**en, ts **ts**etse,
tw **tw**in, uh **a**go, uhr h**er**, v **v**ow, w **w**eather, y **y**oung, z **z**one, zh vi**s**ion

Kibzaim	kib-zay′im
Kidon	k*i*′duhn
Kidron	kid′ruhn
Kilan	k*i*′luhn
Kileab	kil′ee-ab
Kilion	kil′ee-uhn
Kilmad	kil′mad
Kimham	kim′ham
Kinah	k*i*′nuh
King	king
Kinnereth	kin′uh-reth
Kios	k*i*′os
Kir	kihr
Kir-haraseth	kihr-hair′uh-seth
Kir Haraseth	kihr-hair′uh-seth
Kirhareseth	kihr-hair′uh-seth
Kir-hareseth	kihr-hair′uh-seth
Kir Hareseth	kihr-hair′uh-seth
Kir-haresh	kihr-hair′ish
Kirheres	kihr-hihr′iz
Kir-heres	kihr-hihr′iz
Kiriath	kihr′ee-ath
Kiriathaim	kihr′ee-uh-thay′im
Kiriatharba	kihr′ee-ath-ahr′buh
Kiriath-arba	kihr′ee-ath-ahr′buh
Kiriath Arba	kihr′ee-ath-ahr′buh
Kiriatharim	kihr′ee-ath-air′im
Kiriath-arim	kihr′ee-ath-air′im
Kiriathbaal	kihr′ee-ath-bay′uhl
Kiriath-baal	kihr′ee-ath-bay′uhl
Kiriath Baal	kihr′ee-ath-bay′uhl
Kiriathhuzoth	kihr′ee-ath-hy*oo*′zoth
Kiriath-huzoth	kihr′ee-ath-hy*oo*′zoth
Kiriath Huzoth	kihr′ee-ath-hy*oo*′zoth
Kiriathiarius	kihr′ee-ath-ee-air′ee-uhs
Kiriathjearim	kihr′ee-ath-jee′uh-rim
Kiriath-jearim	kihr′ee-ath-jee′uh-rim
Kiriath Jearim	kihr′ee-ath-jee′uh-rim
Kiriathsannah	kihr′ee-ath-san′uh
Kiriath-sannah	kihr′ee-ath-san′uh
Kiriath Sannah	kihr′ee-ath-san′uh
Kiriathsepher	kihr′ee-ath-see′fuhr
Kiriath-sepher	kihr′ee-ath-see′fuhr
Kiriath Sepher	kihr′ee-ath-see′fuhr
Kirioth	kihr′ee-oth

a cat, ah father, ahr lard, air care, aw jaw, ay pay, b bug, ch chew, d do,
e, eh pet, ee seem, er error, f fun, g good, h hot, hw whether, i it, *i* sky,
ihr ear, j joke, k king, kh ch as in German Buch, ks vex, kw quill, l love, m mat,

Kirjath	kihr'jath
Kirjathaim	kihr'juh-thay'im
Kirjath-arba	kihr'jath-ahr'buh
Kirjath Arba	kihr'jath-ahr'buh
Kirjath-arim	kihr'jath-air'im
Kirjath Arim	kihr'jath-air'im
Kirjath-baal	kihr'jath-bay'uhl
Kirjath Baal	kihr'jath-bay'uhl
Kirjath-huzoth	kihr'jath-hy*oo*'zoth
Kirjath Huzoth	kihr'jath-hy*oo*'zoth
Kirjath-jearim	kihr'jath-jee'uh-rim
Kirjath Jearim	kihr'jath-jee'uh-rim
Kirjath-sannah	kihr'jath-san'uh
Kirjath Sannah	kihr'jath-san'uh
Kirjath-sepher	kihr'jath-see'fuhr
Kirjath Sepher	kihr'jath-see'fuhr
Kish	kish
Kishi	kish'*i*
Kishion	kish'ee-uhn
Kishon	k*i*'shon
Kislev	kis'lev
Kislon	kis'lon
Kisloth-tabor	kis'loth-tay'buhr
Kisloth Tabor	kis'loth-tay'buhr
Kison	k*i*'son
Kithlish	kith'lish
Kitlish	kit'lish
Kitron	kit'ron
Kittim	kit'im
Kiyyun	k*i*'yuhn
knop	nop
Koa	koh'uh
Kohath	koh'hath
Kohathite	koh'huh-th*i*t
Koheleth	koh-hel'ith
Kola	koh'luh
Kolaiah	koh-lay'yuh
Kona	koh'nuh
Koph	kohf
kor	kor
Korah	kor'uh
Korahite	kor'uh-h*i*t
Korathite	kor'uh-th*i*t
Korazin	kor-ay'zin
korban	kor'ban

---

n not, ng sing, o hot, oh go, oi boy, oo foot, *oo* boot, oor poor, or for,
ou how, p pat, r run, s so, sh sure, t toe, th thin, *th* then, ts tsetse,
tw twin, uh ago, uhr her, v vow, w weather, y young, z zone, zh vision

Kordan	kor'dan
Kore	kor'ee
Koreite	kor'ee-it
Korhite	kor'hit
koum	koom
Koz	koz
Kub	kuhb
Kue	kyoo'ee
Kulom	kyoo'luhm
kum	koom
Kun	koon
Kushaiah	koo-shay'yuh

L

Laadah	lay'uh-dah
Laadan	lay'uh-dan
Laban	lay'buhn
Labana	luh-bay'nuh
Labaoth	luh-bay'oth
Labo	lay'boh
Laccunus	luh-koo'nuhs
Lacedaemonian	las'uh-di-moh'nee-uhn
Lachish	lay'kish
Lacunus	luh-koo'nuhs
Ladan	lay'duhn
Lael	lay'uhl
Lahad	lay'had
Lahai-roi	luh-hi'roi
Lahai Roi	luh-hi'roi
Lahmam	lah'mam
Lahmas	lah'mahs
Lahmi	lah'mi
Laish	lay'ish
Laishah	lay'i-shah
Lakkum	lak'uhm
Lakum	lay'kuhm
lama	lah'muh
Lamech	lay'mik
lamed	lah'mid
lamedh	lah'mid

---

a cat, ah father, ahr lard, air care, aw jaw, ay pay, b bug, ch chew, d do,
e, eh pet, ee seem, er error, f fun, g good, h hot, hw whether, i it, i sky,
ihr ear, j joke, k king, kh ch as in German Buch, ks vex, kw quill, l love, m mat,

Lamentation	lam′en-tay′shuhn
Laodicea	lay-od′i-see′uh
Laodicean	lay-od′i-see′uhn
Lapidoth	lap′i-doth
Lappidoth	lap′i-doth
Lasaea	luh-see′uh
Lasea	luh-see′uh
Lasha	lay′shuh
Lasharon	luh-shair′uhn
Lasthenes	las′thuh-neez
Latin	lat′in
Lazarus	laz′uh-ruhs
Leah	lee′uh
Leannoth	lee-an′oth
Lebana	li-bay′nuh
Lebanah	li-bay′nuh
Lebanon	leb′uh-nuhn
Lebaoth	li-bay′oth
Lebbaeus	li-bee′uhs
Lebbeus	li-bee′uhs
Leb-kamai	leb′kuh-mi′
Leb Kamai	leb′kuh-mi′
Lebo-hamath	lee′boh-hay′muhth
Lebo Hamath	lee′boh-hay′muhth
Lebonah	li-boh′nah
Lecah	lee′kuh
Legion	lee′juhn
Lehab	lee′hab
Lehabim	li-hay′bim
Lehabite	li-hay′bit
Lehem	lee′hem
Lehi	lee′hi
lema	luh-mah′
Lemuel	lem′yoo-uhl
Leshem	lee′shem
lethech	lee′thik
lethek	lee′thik
Lettus	let′uhs
Letushim	li-too′shim
Letushite	li-too′shit
Leummim	lee-uh′mim
Leummite	lee-uh′mit
Leumonite	lee-oom′uh-nit
Levi	lee′vi
Leviathan	li-vi′uh-thuhn

n not, ng sing, o hot, oh go, oi boy, oo foot, *oo* boot, oor poor, or for,
ou how, p pat, r run, s so, sh sure, t toe, th thin, *th* then, ts tsetse,
tw twin, uh ago, uhr her, v vow, w weather, y young, z zone, zh vision

Levis	lee'vis
Levite	lee'vit
Levitical	li-vit'i-kuhl
Leviticus	li-vit'i-kuhs
Libertine	lib'uhr-teen
Libnah	lib'nuh
Libnath	lib'nath
Libni	lib'ni
Libnite	lib'nit
Libre Hayamim	lib'ri-hay'yuh-mim
Libya	lib'ee-uh
Libyan	lib'ee-uhn
Lidebir	lid'uh-bihr
Likhi	lik'hi
Lilith	lil'ith
Linus	li'nuhs
Lo-ammi	loh-am'i
Lod	lod
Lodebar	loh-dee'buhr
Lo-debar	loh-dee'buhr
Lo Debar	loh-dee'buhr
Lo Debar Karnaim	loh-dee'buhr-kahr-nay'im
Lois	loh'is
Lord	lord
Lo-ruhama	loh'roo-hah'muh
Lo-ruhamah	loh'roo-hah'muh
Lot	lot
Lotan	loh'tan
Lothasubus	loh-thah'suh-buhs
Lozon	loh'zon
Lubim	loo'bim
Lucas	loo'kuhs
Lucifer	loo'si-fuhr
Lucius	loo'shuhs
Lud	luhd
Ludim	loo'dim
Ludite	loo'dit
Luhith	loo'hith
Luke	look
Luz	luhz
Lycaonia	lik'uh-oh'nee-uh
Lycaonian	lik'uh-oh'nee-uhn
Lycia	lish'uh
Lydda	lid'uh
Lydia	lid'ee-uh

a cat, ah father, ahr lard, air care, aw jaw, ay pay, b bug, ch chew, d do,
e, eh pet, ee seem, er error, f fun, g good, h hot, hw whether, i it, *i* sky,
ihr ear, j joke, k king, kh **ch** as in German *Buch*, ks vex, kw quill, l love, m mat,

Lydian	lid'ee-uhn
Lysanias	li-say'nee-uhs
Lysias	lis'ee-uhs
Lysimachus	l*i*-sim'uh-kuhs
Lystra	lis'truh

M

Maacah	may'uh-kuh
Maacath	may'uh-kath
Maacathite	may-ak'uh-th*i*t
Maachah	may'uh-kuh
Maachathi	may-ak'uh-th*i*
Maachathite	may-ak'uh-th*i*t
Maadai	may'uh-d*i*
Maadiah	may'uh-d*i*'uh
Maai	may'*i*
Maaleh-acrabbim	may'uh-leh-uh-krab'im
Maani	may'uh-n*i*
Maarath	may'uh-rath
Maareh-geba	may'uh-ri-gee'buh
Maasai	may'uh-s*i*
Maaseiah	may'uh-see'yah
Maasiai	may-as'ee-*i*
Maasias	may-as'ee-uhs
Maasmas	may-as'muhs
Maath	may'ath
Maaz	may'az
Maaziah	may'uh-z*i*'-uh
Mabdai	mab'd*i*
Macalon	muh-kal'uhn
Macbannai	mak'buh-n*i*
Macbenah	mak-bee'nuh
Maccabee	mak'uh-bee
Maccabeus	mak'uh-bee'uhs
Macedon	mas'uh-don
Macedonia	mas'uh-doh'nee-uh
Macedonian	mas'uh-doh'nee-uhn
Machabee	mak'uh-bee
Machabeus	mak'uh-bee'uhs
Machbanai	mak'buh-n*i*

n not, ng sing, o hot, oh go, oi boy, oo foot, *oo* boot, oor poor, or for,
ou how, p pat, r run, s so, sh sure, t toe, th thin, *th* then, ts tsetse,
tw twin, uh ago, uhr her, v vow, w weather, y young, z zone, zh vision

Machbannai	mak-ban'*i*
Machbena	mak-bee'nuh
Machbenah	mak-bee'nuh
Machi	may'k*i*
Machir	may'kihr
Machirite	may'kuh-r*i*t
Machmas	mak'muhs
Machnadebai	mak-nad'uh-b*i*
Machpelah	mak-pee'luh
Macnadebai	mak-nad'uh-b*i*
Macron	may'kron
Madai	may'd*i*
Madiabun	muh-d*i*'uh-buhn
Madian	may'dee-uhn
Madmannah	mad-man'uh
Madmen	mad'muhn
Madmenah	mad-mee'nuh
Madon	may'don
Maelus	may'uh-luhs
Mag	mag
Magadan	mag'uh-dan
Magbish	mag'bish
Magdala	mag'duh-luh
Magdal-eder	mag'duhl-ee'duhr
Magdalen	mag'duh-luhn
Magdalene	mag'duh-leen
Magdiel	mag'dee-uhl
Maged	may'gid
Magi	may'j*i*
Magog	may'gog
Magor-missabib	may'gor-mis'uh-bib
Magpiash	mag'pee-ash
Magus	may'guhs
Mahalab	may'huh-lab
Mahalah	may'huh-lah
Mahalaleel	muh-hay'luh-lee'uhl
Mahalalel	muh-hal'uh-luhl
Mahalath	may'huh-lath
Mahalath-leannoth	may'huh-lath-lee-an'oth
Mahalath Leannoth	may'huh-lath-lee-an'oth
Mahaleb	may'huh-leb
Mahali	mah'huh-l*i*
Mahanaim	may'huh-nay'im
Mahanath	may'huh-nath
Mahanehdan	may'hun-uh-dan'

a cat, ah father, ahr lard, air care, aw jaw, ay pay, b bug, ch chew, d do,
e, eh pet, ee seem, er error, f fun, g good, h hot, hw whether, i it, *i* sky,
ihr ear, j joke, k king, kh ch as in German Buch, ks vex, kw quill, l love, m mat,

Mahaneh-dan	may'hun-uh-dan'
Mahaneh Dan	may'hun-uh-dan'
Maharai	may'huh-r*i*
Mahath	may'hath
Mahavite	may'huh-v*i*t
Mahazioth	muh-hay'zee-oth
Mahershalalhashbaz	may'huhr-shal'al-hash'baz
Maher-shalal-hash-baz	may'huhr-shal'al-hash'baz
Mahlah	mah'luh
Mahli	mah'l*i*
Mahlite	mah'l*i*t
Mahlon	mah'lon
Mahol	may'hol
Mahseiah	mah-see'yah
Maianeas	may-an'ee-uhs
Makaz	may'kaz
Maked	may'kid
Makheloth	mak-hee'loth
Maki	may'k*i*
Makir	may'kihr
Makirite	may'kuh-r*i*t
Makkedah	muh-kee'duh
Maktesh	mak'tesh
Malachi	mal'uh-k*i*
Malachias	mal'uh-k*i*'uhs
Malachy	mal'uh-kee
Malcam	mal'kam
Malcham	mal'kam
Malchiah	mal-k*i*'uh
Malchiel	mal'kee-uhl
Malchielite	mal'kee-uh-l*i*t
Malchijah	mal-k*i*'juh
Malchiram	mal-k*i*'ruhm
Malchishua	mal'k*i*-sh*oo*'uh
Malchi-shua	mal'k*i*-sh*oo*'uh
Malchus	mal'kuhs
Maleleel	muh-lee'lee-uhl
Malkiel	mal'kee-uhl
Malkielite	mal'kee-uh-l*i*t
Malkijah	mal-k*i*'juh
Malkiram	mal-k*i*'ruhm
Malkishua	mal'k*i*-sh*oo*'uh
Malki-shua	mal'k*i*-sh*oo*'uh
Mallos	mal'uhs
Mallothi	mal'uh-th*i*

n **n**ot, ng si**ng**, o h**o**t, oh g**o**, oi b**oy**, oo f**oo**t, *oo* b**oo**t, oor p**oor**, or f**or**,
ou h**ow**, p **p**at, r **r**un, s **s**o, sh **s**ure, t **t**oe, th **th**in, *th* **th**en, ts **ts**etse,
tw **tw**in, uh **a**go, uhr h**er**, v **v**ow, w **w**eather, y **y**oung, z **z**one, zh vi**s**ion

Malluch	mal′uhk
Malluchi	mal′uh-k*i*
Mallus	mal′uhs
Malta	mawl′tuh
Mamaias	muh-may′yuhs
Mamdai	mam′d*i*
mammon	mam′uhn
Mamre	mam′ree
Mamuchus	muh-my*oo*′kuhs
Manach	man′ak
Manaen	man′ee-uhn
Manahath	man′uh-hath
Manahathite	man′uh-ha′th*i*t
Manahethite	man′uh-heh′th*i*t
Manasseas	muh-nas′ee-uhs
Manasseh	muh-nas′uh
Manassehite	muh-nas′uh-h*i*t
Manasses	muh-nas′eez
Manassite	muh-nas′*i*t
maneh	may′neh
Mani	may′n*i*
Manius	may′nee-uhs
Manlius	man′lee-uhs
Manna	man′uh
manna	man′uh
Manoah	muh-noh′uh
Manoko	man′uh-koh
Manuhoth	muh-ny*oo*′hoth
Maoch	may′ok
Maon	may′on
Maonite	may′uh-n*i*t
Mara	mair′uh
Marah	mair′uh
Maralah	mahr′uh-luh
maranatha	mair′uh-nath′uh, mahr′uh-nath′uh
maran-atha	mair′uh-nath′uh, mahr′uh-nath′uh
maran atha	mair′uh-nath′uh, mahr′uh-nath′uh
Marcaboth	mahr′kuh-both
Marcus	mahr′kuhs
Mardochai	mahr′duh-k*i*
Mardocheus	mahr′duh-kee′uhs
Marduk	mahr′dy*oo*k
Mareal	may′ree-uhl
Mareshah	muh-ree′shuh
Marimoth	mair′i-moth

---

a cat, ah father, ahr lard, air care, aw jaw, ay pay, b bug, ch chew, d do,
e, eh pet, ee seem, er error, f fun, g good, h hot, hw whether, i it, *i* sky,
ihr ear, j joke, k king, kh ch as in German *Buch*, ks vex, kw quill, l love, m mat,

Marisa	mahr′uh-suh
Mark	mahrk
Marmoth	mahr′moth
Maroth	mair′oth
Mars	mahrz
Marsena	mahr-see′nuh
Martha	mahr′thuh
Mary	mair′ee
Masaloth	mas′uh-loth
Maschil	mas′kil
Mash	mash
Mashal	may′shuhl
Masiah	muh-si′uh
Masias	muh-si′uhs
Maskil	mas′kil
Masman	mas′muhn
Maspha	mas′fuh
Masrekah	mas′ruh-kuh
Massa	mas′uh
Massah	mas′uh
Massaite	mas′ay-it
Masseiah	muh-see′yah
Massias	muh-si′uhs
Mathanias	math′uh-ni′uhs
Mathusala	muh-thoo′suh-luh
Matred	may′trid
Matri	may′tri
Matrite	may′trit
Mattan	mat′uhn
Mattanah	mat′uh-nuh
Mattaniah	mat′uh-ni′uh
Mattatha	mat′uh-thuh
Mattathah	mat′uh-thuh
Mattathiah	mat′uh-thi′uh
Mattathias	mat′uh-thi′uhs
Mattattah	mat′uh-tuh
Mattenai	mat′uh-ni
Matthan	math′an
Matthanias	math′uh-ni′uhs
Matthat	math′at
Matthelas	math′uh-luhs
Matthew	math′yoo
Matthias	muh-thi′uhs
Mattithiah	mat′uh-thi′uh
Mazitias	maz′uh-ti′uhs

n not, ng sing, o hot, oh go, oi boy, oo foot, *oo* boot, oor poor, or for,
ou how, p pat, r run, s so, sh sure, t toe, th thin, *th* then, ts tsetse,
tw twin, uh ago, uhr her, v vow, w weather, y young, z zone, zh vision

Mazzaroth	maz'uh-roth
Meah	mee'uh
Meani	mee-ay'n*i*
Mearah	mee-air'uh
Mebunnai	mi-buhn'*i*
Mecherathite	mi-ker'uh-th*i*t
Meconah	mi-koh'nuh
Medaba	med'uh-buh
Medad	mee'dad
Medan	mee'dan
Mede	meed
Medeba	med'uh-buh
Media	mee'dee-uh
Median	mee'dee-uhn
Mediterranean	med'i-tuh-ray'nee-uhn
Meeda	mi-ee'duh
Megiddo	mi-gid'oh
Megiddon	mi-gid'on
Mehallalel	muh-hal'uh-lel
Mehetabeel	mi-het'uh-bee'uhl
Mehetabel	mi-het'uh-bel
Mehida	mi-h*i*'duh
Mehir	mee'huhr
Meholah	mi-hoh'luh
Meholathite	mi-hoh'luh-th*i*t
Mehujael	mi-hyoo'jay-uhl
Mehuman	mi-hyoo'muhn
Mehunim	mi-hyoo'nim
Mejarkon	mi-jahr'kon
Me-jarkon	mi-jahr'kon
Me Jarkon	mi-jahr'kon
Mekerathite	mi-ker'uh-th*i*t
Mekonah	mi-koh'nuh
Melah	mee'luh
Melakim	mel'uh-kim
Melatiah	mel'uh-t*i*'uh
Melchi	mel'k*i*
Melchiah	mel-k*i*'uh
Melchias	mel-k*i*'uhs
Melchiel	mel'kee-uhl
Melchisedec	mel-kis'uh-dek
Melchishua	mel'k*i*-shoo'uh
Melchi-shua	mel'k*i*-shoo'uh
Melchizedec	mel-kiz'uh-dek
Melea	mee'lee-uh

---

a cat, ah father, ahr lard, air care, aw jaw, ay pay, b bug, ch chew, d do,
e, eh pet, ee seem, er error, f fun, g good, h hot, hw whether, i it, *i* sky,
ihr ear, j joke, k king, kh ch as in German Buch, ks vex, kw quill, l love, m mat,

Melech	mee'lik
Melichu	mel'i-ky*oo*
Melicu	mel'i-ky*oo*
Melita	mel'i-tuh
Melki	mel'k*i*
Melzar	mel'zahr
mem	maym
Memmius	mem'ee-uhs
Memphis	mem'fis
Memucan	mi-my*oo*'kuhn
Menahem	men'uh-hem
Menan	mee'nan
mene	mee'nee
Menelaus	men'uh-lay'uhs
Menestheus	mi-nes'thee-uhs
Meni	muh-nee'
Menna	men'uh
Menuhoth	min-y*oo*'hoth
Menuim	men'y*oo*-im
Meon	mee'on
Meonenim	mee-on'uh-nim
Meonothai	mee-on'oh-th*i*
Mephaath	mi-fay'ath
Mephibosheth	mi-fib'oh-sheth
Merab	mee'rab
Meraiah	mi-ray'yuh
Meraioth	mi-ray'yoth
Meran	mer'uhn
Merari	mi-rah'r*i*
Merarite	mi-rah'r*i*t
Merathaim	mer'uh-thay'im
Mercurius	muhr-kyoor'ee-uhs
Mered	mee'rid
Meremoth	mer'uh-moth
Meres	mee'reez
Meribah	mer'i-bah
Meribah-kadesh	mer'i-buh-kay'dish
Meribah Kadesh	mer'i-buh-kay'dish
Meribath	mer'i-bath
Meribathkadesh	mer'i-buhth-kay'dish
Meribath-kadesh	mer'i-buhth-kay'dish
Meribbaal	mer'ib-bay'uhl
Merib-baal	mer'ib-bay'uhl
Merib Baal	mer'ib-bay'uhl
Meriboth	mer'i-both

n **not**, ng **sing**, o **hot**, oh **go**, oi **boy**, oo **foot**, *oo* **boot**, oor **poor**, or **for**,
ou **how**, p **pat**, r **run**, s **so**, sh **sure**, t **toe**, th **thin**, *th* **then**, ts **tsetse**,
tw **twin**, uh **ago**, uhr **her**, v **vow**, w **weather**, y **young**, z **zone**, zh **vision**

Merob	mee'rob
Merodach	mi-roh'dak
Merodachbaladan	mi-roh'dak-bal'uh-duhn
Merodach-baladan	mi-roh'dak-bal'uh-duhn
Merom	mee'rom
Meron	mee'ron
Meronoth	mi-ron'oth
Meronothite	mi-ron'oh-th*i*t
Meroz	mee'roz
Merran	mer'uhn
Meruth	mee'ruhth
Mesaloth	mes'uh-loth
Mesech	mee'sik
Mesha	mee'shuh
Meshach	mee'shak
Meshech	mee'shek
Meshek	mee'shek
Meshelemiah	mi-shel'uh-m*i*'uh
Meshezabeel	mi-shez'uh-bee-uhl
Meshezabel	mi-shez'uh-bel
Meshillemith	mi-shil'uh-mith
Meshillemoth	mi-shil'uh-moth
Meshobab	mi-shoh'bab
Meshullam	mi-sh*oo*l-uhm
Meshullemeth	mi-sh*oo*l'uh-mith
Mesobaite	mi-soh'bay-*i*t
Mesopotamia	mes'uh-puh-tay'mee-uh
Mesraim	mes-ray'im
Messiah	muh-s*i*'uh
Messias	muh-s*i*'uhs
Meterus	muh-tee'ruhs
Methegammah	mee'thig-am'uh
Metheg-ammah	mee'thig-am'uh
Metheg Ammah	mee'thig-am'uh
Methegh-ammah	mee'thig-am'uh
Methoar	mi-thoh'ahr
Methusael	mi-th*oo*'say-uhl
Methuselah	mi-th*oo*'suh-luh
Methushael	mi-th*oo*'shay-uhl
Meunim	mi-y*oo*'nim
Meunite	mi-y*oo*'n*i*t
Mezahab	mee'zuh-hab
Me-zahab	mee'zuh-hab
Mezobaite	mi-zoh'bay-*i*t
Mezobian	mi-zoh'bee-uhn

---

a cat, ah father, ahr lard, air care, aw jaw, ay pay, b bug, ch chew, d do,
e, eh pet, ee seem, er error, f fun, g good, h hot, hw whether, i it, *i* sky,
ihr ear, j joke, k king, kh ch as in German *Buch*, ks vex, kw quill, l love, m mat,

Miamin	m*i*'uh-min
Mibhar	mib'hahr
Mibsam	mib'sam
Mibzar	mib'zahr
Mica	m*i*'kuh
Micah	m*i*'kuh
Micaiah	mi-kay'yuh
Micha	m*i*'kuh
Michael	m*i*'kay-uhl
Michah	m*i*'kuh
Michaiah	mi-kay'yuh
Michal	m*i*'kuhl
Micheas	mik'ee-uhs
Michmas	mik'mas
Michmash	mik'mash
Michmethah	mik'muh-thuh
Michmethath	mik'muh-thath
Michri	mik'r*i*
Michtam	mik'tam
Micmash	mik'mash
Micmethath	mik'muh-thath
Micri	mik'r*i*
Middin	mid'uhn
Midian	mid'ee-uhn
Midianite	mid'ee-uh-n*i*t
Midianitish	mid'ee-uh-n*i*t-ish
midrash	mid'rash
Migdal-eder	mig'duhl-ee'duhr
Migdal Eder	mig'duhl-ee'duhr
Migdalel	mig'duhl-el'
Migdal-el	mig'duhl-el'
Migdal El	mig'duhl-el'
Migdalgad	mig'duhl-gad'
Migdal-gad	mig'duhl-gad'
Migdal Gad	mig'duhl-gad'
Migdal-shechem	mig'duhl-shek'uhm
Migdol	mig'dol
Migron	mig'ron
Mijamin	mij'uh-min
Mikloth	mik'loth
Mikneiah	mik-nee'yah
Miktam	mik'tam
Milalai	mil'uh-l*i*
Milcah	mil'kuh
Milcham	mil'kam

n **n**ot, ng si**ng**, o h**o**t, oh g**o**, oi b**oy**, oo f**oo**t, *oo* b**oo**t, oor p**oo**r, or f**or**,
ou h**ow**, p **p**at, r **r**un, s **s**o, sh **s**ure, t **t**oe, th **th**in, *th* **th**en, ts **ts**etse,
tw **tw**in, uh **a**go, uhr h**er**, v **v**ow, w **w**eather, y **y**oung, z **z**one, zh vi**s**ion

Milcom	mil'kuhm
Miletum	m*i*-lee'tuhm
Miletus	m*i*-lee'tuhs
Millo	mil'oh
mina	min'uh
Miniamin	min'yuh-min
Minjamin	min'juh-min
Minni	min'*i*
Minnith	min'ith
Miphkad	mif'kad
Miriam	mihr'ee-uhm
Mirma	mihr'muh
Mirmah	mihr'muh
Misach	mis'ak
Misael	mis'ay-uhl
Misgab	mis'gab
Mishael	mish'ay-uhl
Mishal	m*i*'shuhl
Misham	m*i*'shuhm
Misheal	mish'ee-uhl
Mishle	mish'lee
Mishma	mish'muh
Mishmannah	mish-man'uh
Mishpat	mish'paht
Mishraite	mish'ray-*i*t
Mispar	mis'pahr
Mispereth	mis-pee'rith
Misrephoth	mis'ruh-foth
Misrephothmaim	mis'ruh-foth-may'im
Misrephoth-maim	mis'ruh-foth-may'im
Misrephoth Maim	mis'ruh-foth-may'im
mite	m*i*t
Mithan	mith'uhn
Mithcah	mith'kuh
Mithkah	mith'kuh
Mithnite	mith'n*i*t
Mithredath	mith'ruh-dath
Mithridates	mith'ruh-day'teez
Mitylene	mit'uh-lee'nee
Mizar	m*i*'zahr
Mizpah	miz'puh
Mizpah-gilead	miz'puh-gil'ee-uhd
Mizpar	miz'pahr
Mizpeh	miz'peh
Mizraim	miz-ray'im

a cat, ah father, ahr lard, air care, aw jaw, ay pay, b bug, ch chew, d do,
e, eh pet, ee seem, er error, f fun, g good, h hot, hw whether, i it, *i* sky,
ihr ear, j joke, k king, kh ch as in German *Buch*, ks vex, kw quill, l love, m mat,

Mizzah	miz'uh
Mnason	nay'suhn
Moab	moh'ab
Moabite	moh'uh-b*i*t
Moabitess	moh'uh-b*i*t-es
Moabitish	moh'uh-b*i*t-ish
Moadiah	moh'uh-d*i*'uh
Mochmur	mok'muhr
Modein	moh'deen
Modin	moh'din
Moeth	moh'eth
Moladah	moh'luh-duh
Molech	moh'lek
Molecheth	moh-lek'ith
Moli	moh'l*i*
Molid	moh'lid
Moloch	moh'lok
Momdis	mom'dis
Momdius	mom'dee-uhs
Moosias	moh'uh-s*i*'uhs
Moossias	moh'uh-s*i*'uhs
Morasthite	moh'ruhs-th*i*t
Morastite	moh'ruhs-t*i*t
Mordecai	mor'duh-k*i*
Moreh	mor'eh
Moresheth	mor'uh-sheth
Moreshethgath	mor'uh-sheth-gath'
Moresheth-gath	mor'uh-sheth-gath'
Moresheth Gath	mor'uh-sheth-gath'
Moriah	muh-r*i*'uh
Mosera	moh-see'ruh
Moserah	moh-see'ruh
Moseroth	moh-see'ruhth
Moses	moh'zis
Mosoch	moh'sok
Mosollam	moh-sol'uhm
Mosollamon	moh-sol'uh-muhn
Moza	moh'zuh
Mozah	moh'zuh
Muppim	muh'pim
Mushi	my*oo*'shi
Mushite	my*oo*'sh*i*t
Musri	my*oo*s'r*i*
Muth-labben	my*oo*th-lab'uhn
Muth Labben	my*oo*th-lab'uhn

n not, ng sing, o hot, oh go, oi boy, oo foot, *oo* boot, oor poor, or for,
ou how, p pat, r run, s so, sh sure, t toe, th thin, *th* then, ts tsetse,
tw twin, uh ago, uhr her, v vow, w weather, y young, z zone, zh vision

Myndos	min′dohs
Myndus	min′duhs
Myra	mi′ruh
myriad	mihr′ee-uhd
Mysia	mis′ee-uh
Mysian	mis′ee-uhn

N

Naam	nay′uhm
Naamah	nay′uh-muh
Naaman	nay′uh-muhn
Naamanite	nay′uh-muh-nit
Naamath	nay′uh-muhth
Naamathite	nay′uh-muh-thit
Naamite	nay′uh-mit
Naarah	nay′uh-ruh
Naarai	nay′uh-ri
Naaran	nay′uh-ruhn
Naarath	nay′uh-ruhth
Naashon	nay′uh-shon
Naasson	nay′uh-son
Naathus	nay′uh-thuhs
Nabajoth	nay′buh-joth
Nabal	nay′buhl
Nabariah	nab′uh-ri′uh
Nabarias	nab′uh-ri′uhs
Nabatean	nab′uh-tee′uhn
Nabathite	nab′uh-thit
Naboth	nay′both
Nabuchodonosar	nab′uh-kuh-don′uh-sahr
Nabuchodonosor	nab′uh-kuh-don′uh-sor
Nachon	nay′kon
Nachor	nay′kor
Nacon	nay′kon
Nadab	nay′dab
Nadabath	nad′uh-bath
Nadabatha	nuh-dab′uh-thuh
Nadib	nay′dib
Naggae	nag′ee
Naggai	nag′i

a cat, ah father, ahr lard, air care, aw jaw, ay pay, b bug, ch chew, d do,
e, eh pet, ee seem, er error, f fun, g good, h hot, hw whether, i it, i sky,
ihr ear, j joke, k king, kh ch as in German Buch, ks vex, kw quill, l love, m mat,

Nagge	nag'ee
Nahalal	nay'huh-lal
Nahale-gaash	nay'huh-lee-gay'ash
Nahaliel	nuh-hay'lee-uhl
Nahallal	nuh-hal'uhl
Nahalol	nay'huh-lol
Naham	nay'ham
Nahamani	nay'huh-may'n*i*
Naharai	nay'huh-r*i*
Naharaim	nay'huh-ray'im
Nahari	nay'huh-r*i*
Nahash	nay'hash
Nahath	nay'hath
Nahbi	nah'b*i*
Nahor	nay'hor
Nahshon	nah'shon
Nahum	nay'huhm
Naidus	n*i*'duhs
Naim	naym
Nain	nayn
Naioth	nay'yoth
Nanaea	nuh-nee'uh
Nanaeon	nuh-nee'uhn
Nanea	nuh-nee'uh
Nangae	nan'gee
Naomi	nay-oh'mee
Naphath	nay'fath
Naphathdor	nay'fath-dor'
Naphath-dor	nay'fath-dor'
Napheth	nay'fith
Naphish	nay'fish
Naphisi	naf'i-s*i*
Naphoth	nay'foth
Naphothdor	nay'foth-dor'
Naphoth-dor	nay'foth-dor'
Naphoth Dor	nay'foth-dor'
Naphtali	naf'tuh-l*i*
Naphtalite	naf'tuh-l*i*t
naphthar	naf'thahr
Naphtuh	naf'tuh
Naphtuhim	naf'tuh-him
Naphtuhite	naf'tuh-h*i*t
Narcissus	nahr-sis'uhs
Nasbas	nas'buhs
Nashim	nay'shim

n **n**ot, ng si**ng**, o h**o**t, oh g**o**, oi b**oy**, oo f**oo**t, *oo* b**oo**t, oor p**oor**, or f**or**,
ou h**ow**, p **p**at, r **r**un, s **s**o, sh **s**ure, t **t**oe, th **th**in, *th* **th**en, ts **ts**etse,
tw **tw**in, uh **a**go, uhr h**er**, v **v**ow, w **w**eather, y **y**oung, z **z**one, zh vi**s**ion

Nasith	nay'sith
Nasor	nay'sor
Nathan	nay'thuhn
Nathanael	nuh-than'ay-uhl
Nathaniah	nath'uh-n*i*'uh
Nathanias	nath'uh-n*i*'uhs
Nathanmelech	nay'thuhn-mee'lik
Nathan-melech	nay'thuhn-mee'lik
Naum	nay'uhm
Nave	nayv
Nazarene	naz'uh-reen
Nazareth	naz'uh-rith
Nazarite	naz'uh-r*i*t
Nazirite	naz'uh-r*i*t
Nazorean	naz'uh-ree'uhn
Neah	nee'uh
Neapolis	nee-ap'uh-lis
Neariah	nee'uh-r*i*'uh
Nebai	nee'b*i*
Nebaioth	ni-bay'yoth
Nebajoth	ni-bay'joth
Neballat	ni-bal'uht
Nebat	nee'bat
Nebo	nee'boh
Nebo-sarsekim	nee'boh-sahr'suh-kim
Nebuchadnezzar	neb'uh-kuhd-nez'uhr
Nebuchadrezzar	neb'uh-kuh-drez'uhr
Nebushasban	neb'uh-shas'ban
Nebushazban	neb'uh-shaz'ban
Nebuzaradan	neb'uh-zuh-ray'duhn
Nebuzar-adan	neb'uh-zuh-ray'duhn
Necho	nee'koh
Nechoh	nee'koh
Neco	nee'koh
Necodan	ni-koh'duhn
Nedabiah	ned'uh-b*i*'uh
Neemias	nee'uh-m*i*'uhs
Negeb	neg'eb
Negev	neg'ev
Neginah	neg'i-nuh
Neginoth	neg'i-noth
Nego	nee'goh
Nehelam	ni-hel'uhm
Nehelamite	ni-hel'uh-m*i*t
Nehemiah	nee'huh-m*i*'uh

a cat, ah father, ahr lard, air care, aw jaw, ay pay, b bug, ch chew, d do,
e, eh pet, ee seem, er error, f fun, g good, h hot, hw whether, i it, *i* sky,
ihr ear, j joke, k king, kh ch as in German Buch, ks vex, kw quill, l love, m mat,

Nehemias	nee'huh-m*i*'uhs
Nehemyah	ni-hem'yuh
Nehiloth	nee'huh-loth
Nehum	nee'huhm
Nehushta	ni-hoosh'tuh
Nehushtan	ni-hoosh'tuhn
Neiel	ni-*i*'uhl
Nekeb	nee'keb
Nekoda	ni-koh'duh
Nemuel	nem'y*oo*-uhl
Nemuelite	nem'y*oo*-uh-l*i*t
Nepheg	nee'fig
nephi	nef'*i*
Nephilim	nef'uh-lim
Nephish	nef'ish
Nephishesim	ni-fish'uh-sim
Nephisim	ni-f*i*'sim
Nephtali	nef'tuh-l*i*
Nephthali	nef'thuh-l*i*
Nephthalim	nef'thuh-lim
nephthar	nef'thahr
Nephtoah	nef-toh'uh
Nephushesim	ni-fy*oo*'shuh-sim
Nephusim	ni-fy*oo*'sim
Nephusite	ni-fy*oo*'s*i*t
Nephussim	ni-fy*oo*'sim
Nepthalim	nep'thuh-lim
Ner	nuhr
Neraiah	ni-ray'yuh
Nereus	nee'ri-y*oo*s
Nergal	nuhr'gal
Nergal-sarezer	nuhr'gal-suh-ree'zuhr
Nergal-sar-ezer	nuhr'gal-suh-ree'zuhr
Nergalsharezer	nuhr'gal-shuh-ree'zuhr
Nergal-sharezer	nuhr'gal-shuh-ree'zuhr
Neri	nee'r*i*
Neriah	ni-r*i*'uh
Nerias	ni-r*i*'uhs
Nero	nihr'oh
Netaim	ni-tay'im
Nethaneal	ni-than'ee-uhl
Nethaneel	ni-than'ee-uhl
Nethanel	ni-than'uhl
Nethaniah	neth'uh-n*i*'uh
Nethinim	neth'in-im

n not, ng sing, o hot, oh go, oi boy, oo foot, *oo* boot, oor poor, or for,
ou how, p pat, r run, s so, sh sure, t toe, th thin, *th* then, ts tsetse,
tw twin, uh ago, uhr her, v vow, w weather, y young, z zone, zh vision

Netopha	ni-toh'fuh
Netophah	ni-toh'fuh
Netophathi	ni-tof'uh-th*i*
Netophathite	ni-tof'uh-th*i*t
Neviim	ni-vi-eem'
Nevi'im	ni-vi-eem'
Neziah	ni-z*i*'uh
Nezib	nee'zib
Nibhaz	nib'haz
Nibshan	nib'shan
Nicanor	n*i*-kay'nuhr
Nicodemus	nik'uh-dee'muhs
Nicolaitan	nik'uh-lay'uh-tuhn
Nicolaitane	nik'uh-lay'uh-tayn
Nicolas	nik'uh-luhs
Nicolaus	nik'uh-lay'uhs
Nicopolis	ni-kop'uh-lis
Nidia	nid'ee-uh
Niger	n*i*'guhr
Nile	n*i*l
Nimrah	nim'ruh
Nimrim	nim'rim
Nimrod	nim'rod
Nimshi	nim'sh*i*
Nineve	nin'uh-veh
Nineveh	nin'uh-vuh
Ninevite	nin'uh-v*i*t
Niphis	nif'is
Nisan	n*i*'san
Nisroch	nis'rok
Nissi	nis'ee
nitre	n*i*'tuhr
No	noh
Noadiah	noh'uh-d*i*'uh
Noah	noh'uh
No-amon	noh-am'uhn
Nob	nob
Nobah	noh'buh
Nobai	noh'b*i*
Nod	nod
Nodab	noh'dab
Nodan	noh'dan
Noe	noh'ee
Noeba	noh-ee'buh
Noemi	noh'uh-m*i*

a cat, ah father, ahr lard, air care, aw jaw, ay pay, b bug, ch chew, d do,
e, eh pet, ee seem, er error, f fun, g good, h hot, hw whether, i it, *i* sky,
ihr ear, j joke, k king, kh ch as in German Buch, ks vex, kw quill, l love, m mat,

Nogah	noh'guh
Nohah	noh'hah
Non	non
Noph	nof
Nophah	noh'fuh
Nubian	ny*oo*'bee-uhn
Numbers	nuhm'buhrz
Numenius	n*oo*-mee'nee-uhs
Nun	nuhn
nun	nuhn
Nympha	nim'fuh
Nymphas	nim'fuhs

O

Obadiah	oh'buh-d*i*'uh
Obal	oh'buhl
Obdia	ob-d*i*'uh
Obed	oh'bid
Obededom	oh'bid-ee'duhm
Obed-edom	oh'bid-ee'duhm
Obeth	oh'bith
Obil	oh'bil
Oboth	oh'both
Ochiel	oh-k*i*'uhl
Ochran	ok'ruhn
Ocidelus	oh-si-dee'luhs
Ocina	oh-s*i*'nuh
Ocran	ok'ruhn
Oded	oh'did
Odollam	oh-dol'uhm
Odomera	od'uh-mer'uh
Odonarkes	od'uh-nahr'keez
Og	og
Ohad	oh'had
Ohel	oh'hel
Oholah	oh-hoh'luh
Oholiab	oh-hoh'lee-ab
Oholibah	oh-hoh'li-buh
Oholibamah	oh-hoh'li-bah'muh
Olamus	oh'luh-muhs

---

n **not**, ng **sing**, o **hot**, oh **go**, oi **boy**, oo **foot**, *oo* **boot**, oor **poor**, or **for**,
ou **how**, p **pat**, r **run**, s **so**, sh **sure**, t **toe**, th **thin**, *th* **then**, ts **tsetse**,
tw **twin**, uh **ago**, uhr **her**, v **vow**, w **weather**, y **young**, z **zone**, zh **vision**

Olive	ol'iv
Olivet	ol'i-vet
Olympas	oh-lim'puhs
Olympian	oh-lim'pee-uhn
Omaerus	oh-mee'ruhs
Omar	oh'mahr
omega	oh-meg'uh
omer	oh'muhr
omerful	oh'muhr-fool
Omri	om'r*i*
On	on
Onam	oh'nuhm
Onan	oh'nuhn
Onesimus	oh-nes'uh-muhs
Onesiphorus	on'uh-sif'uh-ruhs
Oni	oh'n*i*
Onias	oh-n*i*'uhs
Ono	oh'noh
Onus	oh'nuhs
onycha	on'i-kuh
Ophel	oh'fel
Ophir	oh'fuhr
Ophni	of'n*i*
Ophrah	of'ruh
Oracle	or'uh-kuhl
Oreb	or'eb
Oregim	oh'ruh-gim
Oren	or'en
Orion	oh-r*i*'uhn
Ornan	or'nuhn
Orpah	or'puh
Orthosia	or-thoh'see-uh
Orthosias	or-thoh'see-uhs
Osaias	oh-say'yuhs
Osea	oh-see'uh
Oseas	oh-see'uhs
Osee	oh'see
Oshea	oh-shee'uh
Osnappar	os-nap'uhr
Osnapper	os-nap'uhr
Othni	oth'n*i*
Othniel	oth'nee-uhl
Othoniah	oth'uh-n*i*'uh
Othonias	oth'uh-n*i*'uhs
Ox	ohks

a cat, ah father, ahr lard, air care, aw jaw, ay pay, b bug, ch chew, d do,
e, eh pet, ee seem, er error, f fun, g good, h hot, hw whether, i it, *i* sky,
ihr ear, j joke, k king, kh ch as in German Buch, ks vex, kw quill, l love, m mat,

Ozem	oh'zuhm
Ozias	oh-z*i*'uhs
Oziel	oh'zee-uhl
Ozni	oz'n*i*
Oznite	oz'n*i*t
Ozora	oh-zor'uh

P

Paaneah	pay'uh-nee'uh
Paarai	pay'uh-r*i*
Pacatania	pak'uh-tan'ee-uh
Pachon	pay'kuhn
Padan	pay'duhn
Padan-aram	pay'duhn-air'uhm
Padan Aram	pay'duhn-air'uhm
Paddan	pad'uhn
Paddan-aram	pad'uhn-air'uhm
Paddan Aram	pad'uhn-air'uhm
Padon	pay'duhn
Pagiel	pay'gee-uhl
Pahathmoab	pay'hath-moh'ab
Pahath-moab	pay'hath-moh'ab
Pai	p*i*
Palal	pay'lal
Palestina	pal'uh-st*i*'nuh
Palestine	pal'uh-st*i*n
Palet	pay'lit
Pallu	pal'y*oo*
Palluite	pal'y*oo*-*i*t
Palti	pal't*i*
Paltiel	pal'tee-uhl
Paltite	pal't*i*t
Pamphylia	pam-fil'ee-uh
Pannag	pan'ag
Paphos	pay'fos
parable	pair'uh-buhl
Paraclete	pair'uh-kleet
Paradise	pair'uh-d*i*s
Parah	pay'ruh
Paralipomenon	pair'uh-li-pom'uh-non

---

n **not**, ng **sing**, o **hot**, oh **go**, oi **boy**, oo **foot**, *oo* **boot**, oor **poor**, or **for**,
ou **how**, p **pat**, r **run**, s **so**, sh **sure**, t **toe**, th **thin**, *th* **then**, ts **tsetse**,
tw **twin**, uh **ago**, uhr **her**, v **vow**, w **weather**, y **young**, z **zone**, zh **vision**

Paran	pay'ruhn
Parath	pay'ruhth
Parbar	pahr'bahr
Parmashta	pahr-mash'tuh
Parmenas	pahr'muh-nuhs
Parnach	pahr'nak
Parosh	pay'rosh
Parshandatha	pahr-shan'duh-thuh
parsin	pahr'sin
Parthia	pahr'thee-uh
Parthian	pahr'thee-uhn
Paruah	puh-roo'uh
Parvaim	pahr-vay'im
Parzite	pahr-zit
Pas	pas
Pasach	pay'sak
Paschal	pas'kuhl
Pasdammim	pas-dam'im
Pas-dammim	pas-dam'im
Pas Dammim	pas-dam'im
Paseah	puh-see'uh
Pashhur	pash'huhr
Pashur	pash'uhr
Passover	pas'oh-vuhr
Patara	pat'uh-ruh
Patheus	puh-thee'uhs
Pathros	path'ros
Pathrus	path'ruhs
Pathrusim	puh-throo'sim
Pathrusite	puh-throo'sit
Patmos	pat'muhs
Patrobas	pat'ruh-buhs
Patroclus	puh-troh'kluhs
Pau	pou
Paul	pawl
Paulus	paw'luhs
Pazzez	paz'iz
pe	pay
Pedahel	ped'uh-hel
Pedahzur	pi-dah'zuhr
Pedaiah	pi-day'yuh
peh	pay
Pekah	pee'kuh
Pekahiah	pek'uh-hi'uh
Pekod	pee'kod

---

a cat, ah father, ahr lard, air care, aw jaw, ay pay, b bug, ch chew, d do,
e, eh pet, ee seem, er error, f fun, g good, h hot, hw whether, i it, *i* sky,
ihr ear, j joke, k king, kh ch as in German Buch, ks vex, kw quill, l love, m mat,

Pelaiah	pi-lay'yuh
Pelaliah	pel'uh-li'uh
Pelatiah	pel'uh-ti'uh
Peleg	pee'lig
Pelet	pee'lit
Peleth	pee'lith
Pelethite	pel'uh-th*i*t
Pelias	pel'ee-uhs
Pelon	pee'luhn
Pelonite	pel'uh-n*i*t
Pelusium	pi-l*oo*'see-uhm
Peniel	pen'ee-uhl
Peninnah	pi-nin'uh
Pentapolis	pen-tap'uh-lis
Pentecost	pen'ti-kost
Penuel	peh-ny*oo*-uhl
Peor	pee'or
Perath	pee'rath
Perazim	pi-ray'zim
perdition	puhr-di'shuhn
peres	pee'res
Peresh	pee'rish
Perez	pee'riz
Perezite	per'uh-z*i*t
Perezuzza	pee'riz-uh'zuh
Perez-uzza	pee'riz-uh'zuh
Perezuzzah	pee'riz-uh'zuh
Perez-uzzah	pee'riz-uh'zuh
Perez Uzzah	pee'riz-uh'zuh
Perga	puhr'guh
Pergamos	puhr'guh-muhs
Pergamum	puhr'guh-muhm
Perida	pi-r*i*'duh
Perizzite	per'i-z*i*t
Persepolis	puhr-sep'uh-lis
Perseus	puhr'see-uhs
Persia	puhr'zhuh
Persian	puhr'zhuhn
Persis	puhr'sis
Peruda	pi-r*oo*'duh
Peter	pee'tuhr
Pethahiah	peth'uh-h*i*'uh
Pethor	pee'thor
Pethuel	pi'thy*oo*'uhl
Peullethai	pi-*oo*l'uh-th*i*

---

n not, ng sing, o hot, oh go, oi boy, oo foot, *oo* boot, oor poor, or for,
ou how, p pat, r run, s so, sh sure, t toe, th thin, *th* then, ts tsetse,
tw twin, uh ago, uhr her, v vow, w weather, y young, z zone, zh vision

Peulthai	pi-*ool*'th*i*
Phaath Moab	fay'ath-moh'ab
Phacareth	fak'uh-rith
Phadoura	fuh-door'uh
Phaisur	fay'zuhr
Phalaris	fal'uh-ruhs
Phaldaius	fal-day'uhs
Phaleas	fuh-lee'uhs
Phalec	fay'lik
Phallu	fal'*oo*
Phalti	fal't*i*
Phaltiel	fal'tee-uhl
Phanuel	fuh'ny*oo*'uhl
Pharakim	fair'uh-kim
Pharaoh	fair'oh
Pharaoh-hophra	fair'oh-hof'ruh
Pharaoh-necho	fair'oh-nee'koh
Pharaoh-nechoh	fair'oh-nee'koh
Pharaoh-neco	fair'oh-nee'koh
Pharaoh Neco	fair'oh-nee'koh
Pharathon	fair'uh-thon
Pharathoni	fair'uh-thoh'n*i*
Phares	fair'is
Pharez	fair'iz
Pharira	fuh-r*i*'ruh
Pharisaic	fair'uh-say'ik
Pharisee	fair'uh-see
Pharosh	fay'rosh
Pharpar	fahr'pahr
Pharzite	fahr'z*i*t
Phaseah	fuh-see'uh
Phaselis	fuh-see'lis
Phasiron	fas'uh-ron
Phassaron	fas'uh-ron
Phebe	fee'bee
Phelet	fee'lit
Phenice	fi-n*i*'see
Phenicia	fi-ni'shee-uh
Pherezite	fer'uh-z*i*t
Phibeseth	f*i*'buh-seth
Phichol	f*i*'kol
Phicol	f*i*'kol
Philadelphia	fil'uh-del'fee-uh
Philarches	fil-ahr'keez
Philemon	fi-lee'muhn

---

a cat, ah father, ahr lard, air care, aw jaw, ay pay, b bug, ch chew, d do,
e, eh pet, ee seem, er error, f fun, g good, h hot, hw whether, i it, *i* sky,
ihr ear, j joke, k king, kh ch as in German Buch, ks vex, kw quill, l love, m mat,

Philetus	fi-lee'tuhs
Philip	fil'ip
Philippi	fi-lip'*i*, fil'i-p*i*
Philippians	fi-lip'ee-uhnz
Philistia	fi-lis'tee-uh
Philistim	fi-lis'tim
Philistine	fi-lis'teen
Philologus	fil-ol'uh-guhs
Philometor	fil'uh-mee'tor
Philopator	fil'uh-pay'tor
Phineas	fin'ee-uhs
Phinees	fin'ee-uhs
Phinehas	fin'ee-huhs
Phinoi	fin'oi
Phison	f*i*'son
Phlegon	fleg'uhn
Phoebe	fee'bee
Phoenice	fi-n*i*'see
Phoenicia	fi-nish'uh
Phoenician	fi-nish'uhn
Phoenix	fee'niks
Phogor	foh'gor
Phoros	for'os
Phrygia	frij'ee-uh
Phrygian	frij'ee-uhn
Phud	fuhd
Phurah	fyoo'ruh
Phurim	fyoo'rim
Phut	fuht
Phuvah	fyoo'vuh
Phygellus	fi-jel'uhs
Phygelus	f*i*'juh-luhs
phylarch	f*i*'lahrk
Pi	p*i*
Pibeseth	p*i*-bee'sith
Pi-beseth	p*i*-bee'sith
Pi Beseth	p*i*-bee'sith
Pihahiroth	p*i*'huh-h*i*'roth
Pi-hahiroth	p*i*'huh-h*i*'roth
Pi Hahiroth	p*i*'huh-h*i*'roth
Pilate	p*i*'luht
Pildash	pil'dash
Pileha	pil'uh-hah
Pileser	pi-lee'suhr
Pilha	pil'hah

n not, ng sing, o hot, oh go, oi boy, oo foot, *oo* boot, oor poor, or for, ou how, p pat, r run, s so, sh sure, t toe, th thin, *th* then, ts tsetse, tw twin, uh ago, uhr her, v vow, w weather, y young, z zone, zh vision

Pilneser	pil-nee′suhr
Piltai	pil′t*i*
pim	pim
Pinon	p*i*′non
Pira	p*i*′ruh
Piram	p*i*′ruhm
Pirathon	pihr′uh-thon
Pirathonite	pihr′uh-thuh-n*i*t
Pisgah	piz′guh
Pishon	p*i*′shon
Pisidia	pi-sid′ee-uh
Pisidian	pi-sid′ee-uhn
Pisidian Antioch	pi-sid′ee-uhn-an′tee-ok
Pison	p*i*′suhn
Pispa	pis′puh
Pispah	pis′puh
Pithom	p*i*′thom
Pithon	p*i*′thon
Pleiades	plee′uh-deez
Pochereth	pok′uh-rith
Pocherethhazzebaim	pok′uh-rith-haz-uh-bay′im
Pochereth-hazzebaim	pok′uh-rith-haz-uh-bay′im
Pokereth-hazzebaim	pok′uh-rith-haz-uh-bay′im
Pollux	pol′uhks
Pontius	pon′shuhs
Pontus	pon′tuhs
Poratha	por-ay′thuh
Porathai	por-ay′th*i*
Porcius	por′shuhs
Posidonius	pos′i-doh′nee-uhs
Poti	poh′t*i*
Potiphar	pot′uh-fuhr
Potiphera	puh-ti′fuh-ruh
Poti-pherah	puh-ti′fuh-ruh
Praetorian	pri-tor′ee-uhn
Praetorium	pri-tor′ee-uhm
Preacher	pree′chuhr
prefect	pree′fekt
presbyter	pres′bi-tuhr
presbytery	pres′bi-ter′ee
Pretorium	pri-tor′ee-uhm
Prisca	pris′kuh
Priscilla	pri-sil′uh
Prochorus	prok′uh-ruhs
proconsul	proh-kon′suhl

---

a cat, ah father, ahr lard, air care, aw jaw, ay pay, b bug, ch chew, d do,
e, eh pet, ee seem, er error, f fun, g good, h hot, hw whether, i it, *i* sky,
ihr ear, j joke, k king, kh ch as in German *Buch*, ks vex, kw quill, l love, m mat,

proconsular	proh-kon'suh-luhr
Procorus	prok'uh-ruhs
procurator	prok'yuh-ray'tuhr
Prophet	prof'it
proselyte	pros'uh-l*i*t
Proverb	prov'uhrb
Psalm	sahm
psaltery	sawl'tuh-ree
Ptolemaic	tol'uh-may'ik
Ptolemais	tol'uh-may'uhs
Ptolemy	tol'uh-mee
Pua	py*oo*'uh
Puah	py*oo*'uh
publican	puhb'li-kuhn
Publius	puhb'lee-uhs
Pudens	py*oo*'dinz
Puhite	py*oo*'h*i*t
Puite	py*oo*'*i*t
Pul	puhl
Punite	py*oo*'n*i*t
Punon	py*oo*'non
Pur	pyoor
Purah	py*oo*'ruh
Purim	py*oo*'rim
Put	poot
Puteoli	py*oo*-tee'oh-lee
Puthite	py*oo*'th*i*t
Putiel	py*oo*'tee-uhl
Puvah	py*oo*'vuh
Puvahite	py*oo*'vuh-h*i*t
Puvvah	poo'vuh
pygarg	p*i*'gahrg
Pyrrhus	pihr'uhs

Q

Qoheleth	koh-hel'ith
qoph	kohf
quadrans	kwad'ruhns
Quartus	kwor'tuhs
quaternion	kwah-tuhr'nee-uhn

n not, ng sing, o hot, oh go, oi boy, oo foot, *oo* boot, oor poor, or for,
ou how, p pat, r run, s so, sh sure, t toe, th thin, *th* then, ts tsetse,
tw twin, uh ago, uhr her, v vow, w weather, y young, z zone, zh vision

Quintus	kwin'tuhs
Quirinius	kwi-rin'ee-uhs

R

Raama	ray'uh-mah
Raamah	ray'uh-mah
Raamiah	ray'uh-m*i*'uh
Raamses	ray-am'seez
Rab	rab
Rabbah	rab'uh
Rabbath	rab'uhth
rabbi	rab'*i*
Rabbim	rab'im
Rabbith	rab'ith
rabboni	ra-boh'n*i*
rabbouni	ra-b*oo*'n*i*
Rabmag	rab'mag
Rab-mag	rab'mag
Rabsaces	rab'suh-seez
Rabsaris	rab'suh-ris
Rab-saris	rab'suh-ris
Rabshakeh	rab'shuh-kuh
Rab-shakeh	rab'shuh-kuh
raca	rah'kah
Racal	ray'kuhl
Rachab	ray'kab
Rachal	ray'kuhl
Rachel	ray'chuhl
Raddai	rad'*i*
Ragae	ray'gee
Ragau	ray'gaw
Rages	rah'guhs
Raguel	ruh-gy*oo*'uhl
Rahab	ray'hab
Rahab-hem-shebeth	ray'hab-hem-shee'bith
Raham	ray'huhm
Rahel	ray'hel
Rakem	ray'kim
Rakkath	rak'uhth
Rakkon	rak'on

---

a cat, ah father, ahr lard, air care, aw jaw, ay pay, b bug, ch chew, d do,
e, eh pet, ee seem, er error, f fun, g good, h hot, hw whether, i it, *i* sky,
ihr ear, j joke, k king, kh ch as in German *Buch*, ks vex, kw quill, l love, m mat,

Ram	ram
Rama	ray′muh
Ramah	ray′muh
Ramath	ray′muhth
Ramathaim	ram′uh-thay′im
Ramathaimzophim	ram′uh-thay′im-zoh′fim
Ramathaim-zophim	ram′uh-thay′im-zoh′fim
Ramathaim Zophim	ram′uh-thay′im-zoh′fim
Ramathem	ram′uh-thim
Ramathite	ray′muh-th*i*t
Ramathlehi	ray′muhth-lee′h*i*
Ramath-lehi	ray′muhth-lee′h*i*
Ramath Lehi	ray′muhth-lee′h*i*
Ramath-mizpah	ray′muhth-miz′puh
Ramath Mizpah	ray′muhth-miz′puh
Ramathmizpeh	ray′muhth-miz′puh
Ramath-mizpeh	ray′muhth-miz′puh
Rameses	ram′uh-seez
Ramiah	ruh-m*i*′uh
Ramoth	ray′moth
Ramothgilead	ray′muhth-gil′ee-uhd
Ramoth-gilead	ray′muhth-gil′ee-uhd
Ramoth Gilead	ray′muhth-gil′ee-uhd
Ramoth-negeb	ray′muhth-neg′eb
Ramoth Negev	ray′muhth-neg′ev
Rapha	ray′fuh
Raphael	raf′ay-uhl
Raphah	ray′fuh
Raphaim	raf′ay-im
Raphain	raf′ay-in
Raphia	ruh-f*i*′uh
Raphon	ray′fon
Raphu	ray′fy*oo*
Rasses	ras′eez
Rassis	ras′is
Rassisite	ras′i-s*i*t
Rathamin	rath′uh-min
Rathumus	ruh-thy*oo*′muhs
Razis	ray′zis
Reaia	ree-ay′yuh
Reaiah	ree-ay′yuh
Reba	ree′buh
Rebecca	ri-bek′uh
Rebekah	ri-bek′uh
Recab	ree′kab

n not, ng sing, o hot, oh go, oi boy, oo foot, *oo* boot, oor poor, or for, ou how, p pat, r run, s so, sh sure, t toe, th thin, *th* then, ts tsetse, tw twin, uh ago, uhr her, v vow, w weather, y young, z zone, zh vision

115

Recabite	rek′uh-b*i*t
Recah	ree′kuh
Rechab	ree′kab
Rechabite	rek′uh-b*i*t
Rechah	ree′kuh
Rechokim	rek′oh-kim
Red-sea	red′see′
Red Sea	red′see′
Reelaiah	ree′uh-lay′yuh
Reeliah	ree′uh-li′uh
Reelius	ree′uh-li′uhs
Reesaias	ree′uh-say′yuhs
Regem	ree′guhm
Regemmelech	ree′guhm-mee′lik
Regem-melech	ree′guhm-mee′lik
Rehabiah	ree′huh-b*i*′uh
Rehob	ree′hob
Rehoboam	ree′huh-boh′uhm
Rehoboth	ri-hoh′both
Rehoboth-han-nahar	ri-hoh′both-hahn-nay′hahr
Rehoboth-ir	ri-hoh′both-ihr′
Rehoboth Ir	ri-hoh′both-ihr′
Rehum	ree′huhm
Rei	ree′*i*
Rekem	ree′kuhm
Remaliah	rem′uh-li′uh
Remeth	ree′mith
Remmon	rem′uhn
Remmon-methoar	rem′uhn-meth′oh-ahr
Remphan	rem′fuhn
Rephael	ref′ay-uhl
Rephah	ree′fuh
Rephaiah	ri-fay′yuh
Rephaim	ref′ay-im
Rephaite	ref′ay-*i*t
Rephan	ref′uhn
Rephidim	ref′i-dim
Resaiah	ri-say′yuh
Resen	ree′suhn
resh	raysh
Resheph	ree′shif
Resin	ree′sin
Reu	ree′y*oo*
Reuben	r*oo*′bin
Reubenite	r*oo*′bi-n*i*t

a cat, ah father, ahr lard, air care, aw jaw, ay pay, b bug, ch chew, d do,
e, eh pet, ee seem, er error, f fun, g good, h hot, hw whether, i it, *i* sky,
ihr ear, j joke, k king, kh ch as in German *Buch*, ks vex, kw quill, l love, m mat,

Reuel	roo′uhl
Reumah	roo′muh
Revelation	rev′uh-lay′shuhn
Rezeph	ree′zif
Rezia	ri-zi′uh
Rezin	ree′zin
Rezon	ree′zuhn
Rhegium	ree′jee-uhm
Rhesa	ree′suh
Rhoda	roh′duh
Rhodanite	roh′duh-nit
Rhodes	rohdz
Rhodocus	rod′uh-kuhs
Ribai	ri′bi
Riblah	rib′luh
Rimmon	rim′uhn
Rimmono	ri-moh′nuh
Rimmon-parez	rim′uhn-pay′riz
Rimmonperez	rim′uhn-pee′riz
Rimmon-perez	rim′uhn-pee′riz
Rimmon-perez	rim′uhn-pee′riz
Rinnah	rin′uh
Riphath	ri′fath
Rishathaim	rish′uh-thay′im
Rissah	ris′uh
Rithmah	rith′muh
Rizia	ri-zi′uh
Rizpah	riz′puh
Roboam	roh-boh′uhm
Rodanim	roh′duh-nim
Rogel	roh′guhl
Rogelim	roh′guh-lim
Rohgah	roh′guh
Roi	roi
Roimus	roh′i-muhs
Romamtiezer	roh-mam′ti-ee′zuhr
Romamti-ezer	roh-mam′ti-ee′zuhr
Roman	roh′muhn
Rome	rohm
Rompha	rohm′fuh
Rosh	rosh
Ruben	roo′bin
rue	roo
Rufus	roo′fuhs
Ruhama	roo-hay′muh

---

n not, ng sing, o hot, oh go, oi boy, oo foot, *oo* boot, oor poor, or for,
ou how, p pat, r run, s so, sh sure, t toe, th thin, *th* then, ts tsetse,
tw twin, uh ago, uhr her, v vow, w weather, y young, z zone, zh vision

Ruhamah	r*oo*-hay'muh
Rumah	r*oo*'muh
Ruth	r*oo*th

S

Saba	say'buh
sabachthani	suh-bak'thuh-n*i*
Sabaoth	sab'ay-oth
Sabat	sab'uht
Sabateas	sab'uh-tee'uhs
Sabatus	sab'uh-tuhs
Sabbaias	suh-bay'uhs
Sabban	sab'an
Sabbath	sab'uhth
Sabbatheus	sab'uh-thee'uhs
sabbatical	sa-bat'i-kuhl
Sabbeus	sa-bee'uhs
Sabean	suh-bee'uhn
Sabi	say'b*i*
Sabta	sab'tuh
Sabtah	sab'tuh
Sabteca	sab'tuh-kuh
Sabtecah	sab'tuh-kuh
Sabtecha	sab'tuh-kuh
Sabtechah	sab'tuh-kuh
Sacar	say'kahr
Sachar	say'kahr
Sachia	suh-k*i*'uh
Sadamias	sad'uh-m*i*'uhs
Sadas	say'duhs
Saddeus	sad'ee-uhs
Sadduc	sad'uhk
Sadducee	sad'j*oo*-see
Sadduk	sad'uhk
sadhe	sah'day
Sadoc	say'dok
Sahar	say'hahr
Sais	s*i*s
Sakia	suh-k*i*'uh
Sakkuth	sak'uhth

---

a **cat**, ah **father**, ahr **lard**, air **care**, aw **jaw**, ay **pay**, b **bug**, ch **chew**, d **do**,
e, eh **pet**, ee **seem**, er **error**, f **fun**, g **good**, h **hot**, hw **whether**, i **it**, *i* **sky**,
ihr **ear**, j **joke**, k **king**, kh **ch** as in German *Buch*, ks **vex**, kw **quill**, l **love**, m **mat**,

Sala	say'luh
Salah	say'luh
Salamiel	suh-lay'mee-uhl
Salamis	sal'uh-mis
Salasadai	sal'uh-sad'*i*
Salathiel	suh-lay'thee-uhl
Salcah	sal'kuh
Salchah	sal'kuh
Salecah	sal'uh-kuh
Salem	say'luhm
Salim	say'lim
Sallai	sal'*i*
Sallu	sal'*oo*
Sallumus	sal'uh-muhs
Salma	sal'muh
Salmai	sal'm*i*
Salman	sal'man
Salmon	sal'muhn
Salmone	sal-moh'nee
Salom	say'luhm
Salome	suh-loh'mee
Salt-city	sawlt'sit'ee
Salt-sea	sawlt'see'
Salt Sea	sawlt'see'
Salu	say'l*oo*
Salum	say'luhm
Samael	sam'ay-uhl
Samaias	suh-may'yuhs
Samaria	suh-mair'ee-uh
Samarian	suh-mair'ee-uhn
Samaritan	suh-mair'uh-tuhn
Samatus	suh-may'tuhs
samech	sah'mek
Sameius	suh-mee'yuhs
samekh	sah'mek
Samgar	sam'gahr
Samgarnebo	sam'gahr-nee'boh
Samgar-nebo	sam'gahr-nee'boh
Samgar-nebu	sam'gahr-nee'b*oo*
Sami	say'm*i*
Samis	say'mis
Samlah	sam'luh
Sammus	sam'uhs
Samos	say'mos
Samothrace	sam'uh-thrays

n not, ng sing, o hot, oh go, oi boy, oo foot, *oo* boot, oor poor, or for,
ou how, p pat, r run, s so, sh sure, t toe, th thin, *th* then, ts tsetse,
tw twin, uh ago, uhr her, v vow, w weather, y young, z zone, zh vision

Samothracia	sam'uh-thray'shuh
Sampsames	samp'suh-meez
Samson	sam'suhn
Samuel	sam'yoo-uhl
Sanabassar	san'uh-bas'uhr
Sanabassarus	san'uh-bas'uh-ruhs
Sanasib	san'uh-sib
Sanballat	san-bal'at
Sanhedrin	san-hee'druhn
Sansannah	san-san'uh
Saph	saf
Saphat	say'fat
Saphatias	saf'uh-ti'uhs
Sapheth	say'fith
Saphir	say'fuhr
Sapphira	suh-fi'ruh
Sara	sair'uh
Sarabias	sair'uh-bi'uhs
Sarah	sair'uh
Sarai	sair'i
Saraias	suh-ray'yuhs
Saramel	sair'uh-mel
Saraph	sair'uhf
Sarasadai	sair'uh-sad'i
Sarchedonus	sahr'kuh-doh'nis
Sardeus	sahr-dee'uhs
Sardis	sahr'dis
Sardite	sahr'dit
sardius	sahr'dee-uhs
Sarea	sair'ee-uh
Sarepta	suh-rep'tuh
Sargon	sahr'gon
Sarid	sair'id
Saron	sair'uhn
Sarothie	suh-roh'thee
Sarsechim	sahr'suh-kim
Sar-sekim	sahr'suh-kim
Saruch	sair'uhk
Satan	say'tuhn
Sathrabuzanes	sath'ruh-byoo'zuh-neez
Sathra-buzanes	sath'ruh-byoo'zuh-neez
satrap	say'trap
satrapy	say'truh-pee
Saul	sawl
Savaran	sav'uh-ruhn

a cat, ah father, ahr lard, air care, aw jaw, ay pay, b bug, ch chew, d do,
e, eh pet, ee seem, er error, f fun, g good, h hot, hw whether, i it, *i* sky,
ihr ear, j joke, k king, kh ch as in German *Buch*, ks vex, kw quill, l love, m mat,

Savias	suh-v*i*'uhs
Sceva	see'vuh
Schedia	shuh-d*i*'uh
schin	shin
Scripture	skrip'chuhr
Scythian	sith'ee-uhn
Scythopolis	sith-op'uh-lis
Scythopolitan	sith-uh-pol'i-tuhn
seah	see'uh
Seba	see'buh
Sebam	see'bam
Sebat	see'bat
Secacah	si-kay'kuh
Sechenias	sek'uh-n*i*'uhs
Sechu	see'ky*oo*
Secu	see'ky*oo*
Secundus	si-koon'duhs
Sedecias	sed'uh-k*i*'uhs
Segub	see'guhb
Seir	see'uhr
Seira	see'uh-ruh
Seirah	see'uh-ruh
Seirath	see'uh-rath
Sela	see'luh
Selah	see'luh
selah	see'luh
Sela-hammahlekoth	see'luh-huh-mah'luh-koth
Sela Hammahlekoth	see'luh-huh-mah'luh-koth
Seled	see'lid
Selemia	sel'uh-m*i*'uh
Selemias	sel'uh-m*i*'uhs
Seleucia	si-loo'shuh
Seleucia-by-the-sea	si-loo'shuh-b*i*-thuh-see'
Seleucus	si-loo'kuhs
Sem	sem
Semachiah	sem'uh-k*i*'uh
Semakiah	sem'uh-k*i*'uh
Semei	sem'ee-*i*
Semein	sem'ee-uhn
Semellius	si-mel'ee-uhs
Semis	see'mis
Senaah	suh-nay'uh
Senate	sen'it
Seneh	see'nuh
Senir	see'nuhr

n not, ng sing, o hot, oh go, oi boy, oo foot, *oo* boot, oor poor, or for,
ou how, p pat, r run, s so, sh sure, t toe, th thin, *th* then, ts tsetse,
tw twin, uh ago, uhr her, v vow, w weather, y young, z zone, zh vision

Sennacherib	suh-nak′uh-rib
Senuah	si-ny*oo*′uh
Seorim	see-or′im
Sephar	see′fuhr
Sepharad	sef′uh-rad
Sepharvaim	sef′uhr-vay′im
Sephar-vaim	sef′uhr-vay′im
Sepharvite	sef′uhr-v*i*t
Sephatiah	sef′uh-t*i*′uh
Sephela	suh-fee′luh
Serah	sihr′uh
Seraiah	si-ray′yuh
seraph	ser′uf
seraphim	ser′uh-fim
Sered	sihr′id
Seredite	sihr′uh-d*i*t
Sergius	suhr′jee-uhs
Sergius Paulus	suhr′jee-uhs-paw′luhs
Seron	sihr′on
Serug	sihr′uhg
Sesis	see′sis
Sesthel	ses′thuhl
Seth	seth
Sethur	see′thuhr
Seveneh	suh-ven′uh
Shaalabbin	shay′uh-lab′uhn
Shaalbim	shay-al′bim
Shaalbon	shay-al′bon
Shaalbonite	shay-al′buh-n*i*t
Shaalim	shay′uh-lim
Shaaph	shay′af
Shaaraim	shay′uh-ray′im
Shaashgaz	shay-ash′gaz
Shabbethai	shab′uh-th*i*
Shachia	shuh-k*i*′uh
Shaddai	shad′*i*
Shadday	shad′*i*
Shadrach	shad′rak
Shage	shay′geh
Shagee	shay′gee
Shageh	shay′geh
Shahar	shay′hahr
Shaharaim	shay′huh-ray′im
Shahazimah	shay′huh-z*i*′muh
Shahazumah	shay′huh-z*oo*′muh

---

a cat, ah father, ahr lard, air care, aw jaw, ay pay, b bug, ch chew, d do,
e, eh pet, ee seem, er error, f fun, g good, h hot, hw whether, i it, *i* sky,
ihr ear, j joke, k king, kh ch as in German *Buch*, ks vex, kw quill, l love, m mat,

Shakeh	shay'kuh
Shalal	shay'luhl
Shalem	shay'luhm
Shalim	shay'lim
Shalisha	shuh-li'shuh
Shalishah	shuh-li'shuh
Shallecheth	shal'uh-kith
Shalleketh	shal'uh-kith
Shallum	shal'uhm
Shallun	shal'uhn
Shalmai	shal'mi
Shalman	shal'muhn
Shalmaneser	shal'muh-nee'zuhr
Shalom	shah-lohm'
Shama	shay'muh
Shamariah	sham'uh-ri'uh
Shamed	shay'mid
Shamer	shay'muhr
Shamgar	sham'gahr
Shamhuth	sham'huhth
Shamir	shay'muhr
Shamlai	sham'li
Shamma	sham'uh
Shammah	sham'uh
Shammai	sham'i
Shammoth	sham'oth
Shammua	sha-myoo'uh
Shammuah	sha-myoo'uh
Shamsherai	sham'shuh-ri
Shan	shan
Shapham	shay'fuhm
Shaphan	shay'fuhn
Shaphat	shay'fat
Shapher	shay'fuhr
Shaphir	shay'fuhr
Sharai	shair'i
Sharaim	shuh-ray'im
Sharar	shair'ahr
Sharezer	shuh-ree'zuhr
Sharon	shair'uhn
Sharonite	shair'uh-nit
Sharuhen	shuh-roo'huhn
Shashai	shay'shi
Shashak	shay'shak
Shaul	shawl

---

n **not**, ng **sing**, o **hot**, oh **go**, oi **boy**, oo **foot**, *oo* **boot**, oor **poor**, or **for**, ou **how**, p **pat**, r **run**, s **so**, sh **sure**, t **toe**, th **thin**, *th* **then**, ts **tsetse**, tw **twin**, uh **ago**, uhr **her**, v **vow**, w **weather**, y **young**, z **zone**, zh **vision**

Shaulite	shaw'l*i*t
Shaveh	shay'vuh
Shavehkiriathaim	shay'vuh-kihr-ee-uh-thay'im
Shaveh-kiriathaim	shay'vuh-kihr-ee-uh-thay'im
Shaveh Kiriathaim	shay'vuh-kihr-ee-uh-thay'im
Shavsha	shav'shuh
Shawsha	shaw'shuh
Sheal	shee'uhl
Shealtiel	shee-al'tee-uhl
Shean	shee'uhn
Shear	shee'uhr
Sheariah	shee'uh-r*i*'uh
Shearjashub	shee'uhr-jay'shuhb
Shear-jashub	shee'uhr-jay'shuhb
Shear Jashub	shee'uhr-jay'shuhb
Sheba	shee'buh
Shebah	shee'buh
Shebam	shee'bam
Shebaniah	sheb'uh-n*i*'uh
Shebarim	sheb'uh-rim
Shebat	shee'bat
Sheber	shee'buhr
Shebna	sheb'nuh
Shebnah	sheb'nuh
Shebuel	shi-by*oo*'uhl
Shecaniah	shek'uh-n*i*'uh
Shechaniah	shek'uh-n*i*'uh
Shechem	shek'uhm
Shechemite	shek'uh-m*i*t
Shedeur	shed'ee-uhr
Sheerah	shee'uh-ruh
Shehariah	shee'huh-r*i*'uh
shekel	shek'uhl
Shelah	shee'luh
Shelahite	shee'luh-h*i*t
Shelanite	shee'luh-n*i*t
Shelemiah	shel'uh-m*i*'uh
Sheleph	shee'lif
Shelesh	shee'lish
Shelomi	shi-loh'm*i*
Shelomith	shi-loh'mith
Shelomoth	shi-loh'moth
Shelumiel	shi-*loo*'mee-uhl
Shem	shem
Shema	shee'muh, shuh-mah'

a cat, ah father, ahr lard, air care, aw jaw, ay pay, b bug, ch chew, d do,
e, eh pet, ee seem, er error, f fun, g good, h hot, hw whether, i it, *i* sky,
ihr ear, j joke, k king, kh ch as in German *Buch*, ks vex, kw quill, l love, m mat,

Shemaah	shi-may′uh
Shemaiah	shi-may′yuh
Shemariah	shem′uh-ri′uh
Shemeber	shem-ee′buhr
Shemed	shee′mid
Shemei	shem′ee-i
Shemer	shee′muhr
Shemesh	shem′ish
Shemiah	shi-mi′uh
Shemida	shi-mi′duh
Shemidah	shi-mi′duh
Shemidaite	shi-mi′day-it
Sheminith	shem′uh-nith
Shemiramoth	shi-mihr′uh-moth
Shemite	shem′it
Shemoth	shee′moth
Shemuel	shem′yoo-uhl
Shen	shen
Shenazar	shi-naz′uhr
Shenazzar	shi-naz′uhr
Shenir	shee′nuhr
Sheol	shee′ohl
Shepham	shee′fuhm
Shephathiah	shef′uh-thi′uh
Shephatiah	shef′uh-ti′uh
Shephelah	shi-fee′luh
Shepher	shee′fuhr
Shephi	shee′fi
Shepho	shee′foh
Shephupham	shi-fyoo′fuhm
Shephuphan	shi-fyoo′fuhn
Sherah	shee′ruh
Sherebiah	sher′uh-bi′uh
Sheresh	shihr′ish
Sherezer	shuh-ree′zuhr
Sheshach	shee′shak
Sheshai	shee′shi
Sheshak	shee′shak
Sheshan	shee′shan
Sheshbazzar	shesh-baz′uhr
Sheth	sheth
Shethar	shee′thahr
Shethar-baznai	shee′thahr-bahz′ni
Shetharbozenai	shee′thahr-boz′uh-ni
Shethar-bozenai	shee′thahr-boz′uh-ni

n not, ng sing, o hot, oh go, oi boy, oo foot, *oo* boot, oor poor, or for,
ou how, p pat, r run, s so, sh sure, t toe, th thin, *th* then, ts tsetse,
tw twin, uh ago, uhr her, v vow, w weather, y young, z zone, zh vision

Shethar-boznai	shee'thahr-boz'n*i*
Sheva	shee'vuh
Shibah	sh*i*'buh
shibboleth	shib'uh-lith
Shibmah	shib'muh
Shicron	shik'ron
Shiggaion	shuh-gay'on
Shiggionoth	shig'ee-oh'noth
Shigionoth	shig'ee-oh'noth
Shihon	sh*i*'hon
Shihor	sh*i*'hor
Shihorlibnath	sh*i*'hor-lib'nath
Shihor-libnath	sh*i*'hor-lib'nath
Shihor Libnath	sh*i*'hor-lib'nath
Shikkeron	shik'uh-ron
Shilhi	shil'h*i*
Shilhim	shil'him
Shillem	shil'uhm
Shillemite	shil'uh-m*i*t
Shiloah	sh*i*-loh'uh
Shiloh	sh*i*'loh
Shiloni	shi-loh'n*i*
Shilonite	sh*i*'luh-n*i*t
Shilshah	shil'shuh
Shimea	shim'ee-uh
Shimeah	shim'ee-uh
Shimeam	shim'ee-uhm
Shimeath	shim'ee-ath
Shimeathite	shim'ee-uh-th*i*t
Shimei	shim'ee-*i*
Shimeite	shim'ee-*i*t
Shimeon	shim'ee-uhn
Shimhi	shim'h*i*
Shimi	shim'*i*
Shimite	shim'*i*t
Shimma	shim'uh
Shimon	sh*i*'muhn
Shimrath	shim'rath
Shimri	shim'r*i*
Shimrith	shim'rith
Shimrom	shim'rom
Shimron	shim'ron
Shimronite	shim'ruh-n*i*t
Shimronmeron	shim'ron-mee'ron
Shimron-meron	shim'ron-mee'ron

a cat, ah father, ahr lard, air care, aw jaw, ay pay, b bug, ch chew, d do,
e, eh pet, ee seem, er error, f fun, g good, h hot, hw whether, i it, *i* sky,
ihr ear, j joke, k king, kh ch as in German Buch, ks vex, kw quill, l love, m mat,

Shimron Meron	shim'ron-mee'ron
Shimshai	shim'sh*i*
shin	shin
Shinab	sh*i*'nab
Shinar	sh*i*'nahr
Shion	sh*i*'uhn
Shiphi	sh*i*'f*i*
Shiphmite	shif'm*i*t
Shiphrah	shif'ruh
Shiphtan	shif'tan
Shir Hashirim	shihr'hah'shuh-rim
Shisha	sh*i*'shuh
Shishak	sh*i*'shak
Shitrai	shit'r*i*
Shittah	shit'uh
shittah	shit'uh
Shittim	shi'tim
shittim	shi'tim
Shiza	sh*i*'zuh
Shoa	shoh'uh
Shobab	shoh'bab
Shobach	shoh'bak
Shobai	shoh'b*i*
Shobal	shoh'buhl
Shobek	shoh'bek
Shobi	shoh'b*i*
Shocho	shoh'koh
Shochoh	shoh'koh
Shoco	shoh'koh
Shofetim	shoh'fuh-tim
Shoham	shoh'ham
Shomer	shoh'muhr
Shophach	shoh'fak
Shophan	shoh'fan
Shoshanim	shoh-shan'im
Shoshannim	shoh-shan'im
Shoshannim-eduth	shoh-shan'im-ee'duhth
Shoshannim Eduth	shoh-shan'im-ee'duhth
Shua	sh*oo*'uh
Shuah	sh*oo*'uh
Shual	sh*oo*'uhl
Shubael	sh*oo*'bay-uhl
Shuh	sh*oo*
Shuhah	sh*oo*'huh
Shuham	sh*oo*'ham

n not, ng sing, o hot, oh go, oi boy, oo foot, *oo* boot, oor poor, or for,
ou how, p pat, r run, s so, sh sure, t toe, th thin, *th* then, ts tsetse,
tw twin, uh ago, uhr her, v vow, w weather, y young, z zone, zh vision

Shuhamite	shoo'huh-mit
Shuhite	shoo'hit
Shulamite	shoo'luh-mit
Shulammite	shoo'luh-mit
Shumathite	shoo'muh-thit
Shunamite	shoo'nuh-mit
Shunammite	shoo'nuh-mit
Shunem	shoo'nuhm
Shuni	shoo'ni
Shunite	shoo'nit
Shupham	shoo'fuhm
Shuphamite	shoo'fuh-mit
Shuppim	shuh'pim
Shuppite	shuh'pit
Shur	shoor
Shushan	shoo'shan
Shushanchite	shoo'shan-kit
Shushan-eduth	shoo'shan-ee'duhth
Shushan Eduth	shoo'shan-ee'duhth
Shuthalhite	shoo'thuhl-hit
Shuthelah	shoo'thuh-luh
Shuthelahite	shoo'thuh-luh-hit
Shuthelaite	shoo'thuh-lay-it
Shuthite	shoo'thit
Sia	si'uh
Siaha	si'uh-huh
Sibbecai	sib'uh-ki
Sibbechai	sib'uh-ki
sibboleth	sib'uh-lith
Sibmah	sib'muh
Sibraim	sib'ray-im
Sichem	sik'uhm
Sicyon	sish'ee-uhn
Siddim	sid'im
Side	si'dee
Sidon	si'duhn
Sidonian	si-doh'nee-uhn
Sidrach	sid'rak
Sihon	si'hon
Sihor	si'hor
Sikkuth	sik'uhth
Silas	si'luhs
Silla	sil'uh
Silo	si'loh
Siloah	si-loh'uh

a cat, ah father, ahr lard, air care, aw jaw, ay pay, b bug, ch chew, d do,
e, eh pet, ee seem, er error, f fun, g good, h hot, hw whether, i it, *i* sky,
ihr ear, j joke, k king, kh ch as in German *Buch*, ks vex, kw quill, l love, m mat,

Siloam	s*i*-loh'uhm
Silvanus	sil-vay'nuhs
Simalcue	si-mal'ky*oo*-ee
Simeon	sim'ee-uhn
Simeonite	sim'ee-uh-n*i*t
Simmagir	sim'uh-guhr
Simon	s*i*'muhn
Simon-peter	s*i*'muhn-pee'tuhr
Simon Peter	s*i*'muhn-pee'tuhr
Simri	sim'r*i*
Sin	sin
Sina	s*i*'nuh
Sinai	s*i*'n*i*
Sinim	s*i*n'im
Sinite	sin'*i*t
Sion	s*i*'uhn
Siphmoth	sif'moth
Sippai	sip'*i*
Sira	s*i*'ruh
Sirach	s*i*'ruhk
Sirah	s*i*'ruh
Sirion	sihr'ee-uhn
Sisamai	sis'uh-m*i*
Sisera	sis'uh-ruh
Sisinnes	si-sin'es
Sismai	sis'm*i*
sistrum	sis'troom
Sithri	sith'r*i*
Sitnah	sit'nuh
Sivan	s*i*'van
Siyon	s*i*'yuhn
Smyrna	smuhr'nuh
So	soh
Socho	soh'koh
Sochoh	soh'koh
Soco	soh'koh
Socoh	soh'koh
Sodi	soh'd*i*
Sodom	sod'uhm
Sodoma	sod'uh-muh
Sodomite	sod'uh-m*i*t
Sohar	soh'hahr
Soharite	soh'huh-r*i*t
Solomon	sol'uh-muhn
Sopater	soh'puh-tuhr

n not, ng sing, o hot, oh go, oi boy, oo foot, *oo* boot, oor poor, or for,
ou how, p pat, r run, s so, sh sure, t toe, th thin, *th* then, ts tsetse,
tw twin, uh ago, uhr her, v vow, w weather, y young, z zone, zh vision

Sophar	soh'fahr
Sophereth	sof'uh-rith
Sopherim	sof'uh-rim
Sophonias	sof'uh-ni'uhs
Sorek	sor'ik
Sores	soh'rees
Sosipater	soh'sip'uh-tuhr
Sosthenes	sos'thuh-neez
Sostratus	sos'truh-tuhs
Sotai	soh'ti
Spain	spayn
Sparta	spahr'tuh
Spartan	spahr'tuhn
Spirit	spihr'it
Stachys	stay'kis
stacte	stak'tee
stadia	stay'dee-uh
stater	stay'tuhr
Stephanas	stef'uh-nuhs
Stephen	stee'vuhn
Stoic	stoh'ik
Stoick	stoh'ik
storax	stor'aks
Stygian	sti'jee-uhn
Sua	soo'uh
Suah	soo'uh
Suba	soo'buh
Subai	soo'bi
Subas	soo'buhs
Sucathite	soo'kuh-thit
Succoth	suhk'uhth
Succothbenoth	suhk'uhth-bee'noth
Succoth-benoth	suhk'uhth-bee'noth
Succoth Benoth	suhk'uhth-bee'noth
Suchathite	soo'kuh-thit
Sud	suhd
Sudan	soo'dan
Sudanese	soo'duh-neez
Sudias	soo'dee-uhs
Suez	soo'ez
Sukkiim	suhk'ee-im
Sukkite	suh'kit
Sukkoth	suhk'uhth
Suph	soof
Suphah	soo'fuh

---

a cat, ah father, ahr lard, air care, aw jaw, ay pay, b bug, ch chew, d do,
e, eh pet, ee seem, er error, f fun, g good, h hot, hw whether, i it, i sky,
ihr ear, j joke, k king, kh ch as in German Buch, ks vex, kw quill, l love, m mat,

Sur	soor
Susa	s*oo*'suh
Susah	s*oo*'suh
Susanchite	s*oo*'suhn-k*i*t
Susanna	s*oo*-zan'uh
Susi	s*oo*'s*i*
Susian	s*oo*'see-uhn
Susim	s*oo*'sim
sycamine	sik'uh-meen
Sychar	s*i*'kahr
Sychem	s*i*'kuhm
Syelus	suh-ee'luhs
Syene	s*i*-ee'nee
Symeon	sim'ee-uhn
synagogue	sin'uh-gog
Syntyche	sin'ti-kee
Syracuse	sihr'uh-ky*oo*z
Syria	sihr'ee-uh
Syriack	sihr'ee-ak
Syria-damascus	sihr'ee-uh-duh-mas'kuhs
Syria-maachah	sihr'ee-uh-may'uh-kuh
Syrian	sihr'ee-uhn
Syrophenecian	s*i*'roh-fi-nish'uhn
Syrophoenician	s*i*'roh-fi-nish'uhn
Syro-phoenician	s*i*'roh-fi-nish'uhn
Syrtis	suhr'tuhs

T

Taanach	tay'uh-nak
Taanathshiloh	tay'uh-nath-sh*i*'loh
Taanath-shiloh	tay'uh-nath-sh*i*'loh
Taanath Shiloh	tay'uh-nath-sh*i*'loh
Tabaliah	tab'uh-l*i*'uh
Tabbaoth	tab'ay-oth
Tabbath	tab'uhth
Tabbur-haares	tab'uhr-hay-ahr'es
Tabeal	tab'ee-uhl
Tabeel	tab'ee-uhl
Tabellius	tuh-bel'ee-uhs
Taberah	tab'uh-ruh

n not, ng sing, o hot, oh go, oi boy, oo foot, *oo* boot, oor poor, or for,
ou how, p pat, r run, s so, sh sure, t toe, th thin, *th* then, ts tsetse,
tw twin, uh ago, uhr her, v vow, w weather, y young, z zone, zh vision

Tabernacle	tab'uhr-nak'uhl
Tabitha	tab'i-thuh
Tabor	tay'buhr
tabret	tab'rit
Tabrimmon	tab-rim'uhn
Tabrimon	tab-rim'uhn
tache	tak
Tachemon	tak'i-muhn
Tachmonite	tak'muh-n*i*t
Tadmor	tad'mor
Tahan	tay'han
Tahanite	tay'huh-n*i*t
Tahapanes	tuh-hap'uh-neez
Tahash	tay'hash
Tahath	tay'hath
Tahchemonite	tah-kee'muh-n*i*t
Tahkemonite	tah-kee'muh-n*i*t
Tahpanhes	tah'puhn-heez
Tahpannes	tah'puh-neez
Tahpenes	tah'puh-neez
Tahrea	tah'ree-uh
Tahtim-hodshi	tah'tim-hod'sh*i*
Tahtim Hodshi	tah'tim-hod'sh*i*
talent	tal'uhnt
talitha-cumi	tal'uh-thuh-k*oo*'m*i*
talitha cumi	tal'uh-thuh-k*oo*'m*i*
talitha-koum	tal'uh-thuh-k*oo*m'
Talmai	tal'm*i*
Talmon	tal'muhn
Talsas	tal'suhs
Tamah	tay'muh
Tamar	tay'mahr
tamarisk	tam'uh-risk
Tammuz	tam'uhz
Tanach	tay'nak
Tanak	tay'nak
Tanakh	tay'nak
Tanhumeth	tan-hy*oo*'mith
Tanis	tan'is
Taphath	tay'fath
Taphnes	taf'neez
Taphnez	taf'neez
Taphon	tay'fon
Tappuah	tap'y*oo*-uh
Tarah	tair'uh

a cat, ah father, ahr lard, air care, aw jaw, ay pay, b bug, ch chew, d do,
e, eh pet, ee seem, er error, f fun, g good, h hot, hw whether, i it, *i* sky,
ihr ear, j joke, k king, kh ch as in German *Buch*, ks vex, kw quill, l love, m mat,

132

Taralah	tair'uh-luh
Tarea	tair'ee-uh
Tarpelite	tahr'puh-l*i*t
Tarshish	tahr'shish
Tarshishah	tahr'shuh-shah
Tarsus	tahr'suhs
Tartak	tahr'tak
Tartan	tahr'tan
Tartarus	tahr'tuh-ruhs
Taschith	tas'kith
Tatam	tay'tuhm
Tatnai	tat'n*i*
Tattenai	tat'uh-n*i*
tau	tou
taw	taw
Tebah	tee'buh
Tebaliah	teb'uh-l*i*'uh
Tebeth	tee'bith
Tehaphnehes	tuh-haf'nuh-heez
Tehillim	tuh-hil'im
Tehinnah	tuh-hin'uh
teil	teel
tekel	tek'uhl
Tekoa	tuh-koh'uh
Tekoah	tuh-koh'uh
Tekoite	tuh-koh'*i*t
Tel	tel
Telabib	tel'uh-beeb'
Tel-abib	tel'uh-beeb'
Tel Abib	tel'uh-beeb'
Telah	tee'luh
Telaim	tuh-lay'im
Telam	tee'luhm
Telassar	tel-as'ahr
Tel-assar	tel-as'ahr
Tel Assar	tel-as'ahr
Tel Aviv	tel'uh-veev'
Telem	tee'lim
Tel-haresha	tel'huh-ree'shuh
Tel-harsa	tel-hahr'suh
Telharsha	tel-hahr'shuh
Tel-harsha	tel-hahr'shuh
Tel Harsha	tel-hahr'shuh
Telmelah	tel-mee'luh
Tel-melah	tel-mee'luh

n not, ng sing, o hot, oh go, oi boy, oo foot, *oo* boot, oor poor, or for,
ou how, p pat, r run, s so, sh sure, t toe, th thin, *th* then, ts tsetse,
tw twin, uh ago, uhr her, v vow, w weather, y young, z zone, zh vision

Tel Melah	tel-mee'luh
Tema	tee'muh
Temah	tee'muh
Teman	tee'muhn
Temani	tee'muh-n*i*
Temanite	tee'muh-n*i*t
Temeni	tem'uh-n*i*
Temenite	tem'uh-n*i*t
tenon	ten'uhn
Tephon	tee'fon
Terah	ter'uh
teraphim	ter'uh-fim
terebinth	ter'uh-binth
Teresh	tihr'esh
Tertius	tuhr'shee-uhs
Tertullus	tuhr-tuhl'uhs
Testament	tes'tuh-muhnt
Teta	tay'tuh
teth	teth
tetrarch	tet'rahrk
tetter	tet'uhr
Thaddaeus	thad'ee-uhs
Thaddeus	thad'ee-uhs
Thahash	thay'hash
Thamah	thay'muh
Thamar	thay'mahr
Thammuz	tham'uhz
Thamnatha	tham'nuh-thuh
Thara	thair'uh
Thares	thair'es
Tharra	thair'uh
Tharshish	thahr'shish
Thassi	thas'*i*
Thebes	theebz
Thebez	thee'biz
Thecoe	thuh-koh'ee
Thelasar	thel'uh-sahr
Thelersas	thuh-luhr'suhs
Theman	thee'muhn
Theocanus	thee-ok'uh-nuhs
Theodotus	thee-od'uh-tuhs
Theophilus	thee-of'uh-luhs
Theras	thee'ruhs
Thermeleth	thuhr-mee'lith
Thessalonian	thes'uh-loh'nee-uhn

a cat, ah father, ahr lard, air care, aw jaw, ay pay, b bug, ch chew, d do,
e, eh pet, ee seem, er error, f fun, g good, h hot, hw whether, i it, *i* sky,
ihr ear, j joke, k king, kh ch as in German Buch, ks vex, kw quill, l love, m mat,

Thessalonica	thes'uh-luh-n*i*'kuh
Theudas	th*oo*'duhs
Thimnathah	thim'nuh-thuh
Thisbe	this'bee
Thomas	tom'uhs
Thomoi	thom'oi
Thracian	thray'shee-uhn
Thraseas	thray-see'uhs
Three Taverns	three'tav'uhrns
Thummim	thum'im
Thyatira	thi'uh-t*i*'ruh
thyine	th*i*'in
Tiberias	t*i*-bihr'ee-uhs
Tiberius	t*i*-bihr'ee-uhs
Tibhath	tib'hath
Tibni	tib'n*i*
Ticon	t*i*'kuhn
Tidal	t*i*'duhl
Tiglathpileser	tig'lath-pi-lee'zuhr
Tiglath-pileser	tig'lath-pi-lee'zuhr
Tigris	t*i*'gris
Tikvah	tik'vuh
Tikvath	tik'vath
Tilgathpilneser	til'gath-pil-nee'zuhr
Tilgath-pilneser	til'gath-pil-nee'zuhr
Tilon	t*i*'luhn
Timaeus	t*i*-mee'uhs
Timna	tim'nuh
Timnah	tim'nuh
Timnah-serah	tim'nuh-sihr'uh
Timnath	tim'nath
Timnathheres	tim'nath-hee'riz
Timnath-heres	tim'nath-hee'riz
Timnath Heres	tim'nath-hee'riz
Timnathserah	tim'nath-sihr'uh
Timnath-serah	tim'nath-sihr'uh
Timnath Serah	tim'nath-sihr'uh
Timnite	tim'n*i*t
Timon	t*i*'muhn
Timotheus	ti-moh'thee-uhs
Timothy	tim'oh-thee
Tiphsah	tif'suh
Tiras	t*i*'ruhs
Tirathite	t*i*'ruh-th*i*t
Tirhakah	tuhr-hay'kuh

---

n **n**ot, ng si**ng**, o h**o**t, oh g**o**, oi b**oy**, oo f**oo**t, *oo* b**oo**t, oor p**oor**, or f**or**,
ou h**ow**, p **p**at, r **r**un, s **s**o, sh **s**ure, t **t**oe, th **th**in, *th* **th**en, ts **ts**etse,
tw **tw**in, uh **a**go, uhr h**er**, v **v**ow, w **w**eather, y **y**oung, z **z**one, zh vi**s**ion

Tirhanah	tuhr-hay'nuh
Tiria	tihr'ee-uh
Tirshatha	tuhr-shay'thuh
Tirzah	tihr'zuh
Tishbe	tish'bee
Tishbite	tish'b*i*t
Titan	t*i*'tuhn
Titius	tish'ee-uhs
Titius Justus	tish'ee-uhs-juhs'tuhs
tittle	tit'uhl
Titus	t*i*'tuhs
Tiz	tiz
Tizite	t*i*z'*i*t
Toah	toh'uh
Tob	tob
Tobadonijah	tob'ad-uh-n*i*'juh
Tob-adonijah	tob'ad-uh-n*i*'juh
Tobiad	toh-b*i*'uhd
Tobiah	toh-b*i*'uh
Tobias	toh-b*i*'uhs
Tobie	toh'bee
Tobiel	toh'bee-uhl
Tobijah	toh-b*i*'juh
Tobit	toh'bit
Tochen	toh'kuhn
Togarmah	toh-gahr'muh
Tohu	toh'hy*oo*
Toi	toi
Token	toh'kin
Tokhath	tok'hath
Tola	toh'luh
Tolad	toh'lad
Tolaite	toh'lay-*i*t
Tolbanes	tol'buh-neez
Tophel	toh'fuhl
Tophet	toh'fit
Topheth	toh'fith
Torah	toh'ruh
Tormah	tor'muh
Tou	t*oo*
Toubiani	t*oo*'bee-ay'nee
Trachonitis	trak'uh-n*i*'tis
Traconitis	trak'uh-n*i*'tis
Transeuphrates	trans'y*oo*-fray'teez
Trans-euphrates	trans'y*oo*-fray'teez

a cat, ah father, ahr lard, air care, aw jaw, ay pay, b bug, ch chew, d do,
e, eh pet, ee seem, er error, f fun, g good, h hot, hw whether, i it, *i* sky,
ihr ear, j joke, k king, kh ch as in German *Buch*, ks vex, kw quill, l love, m mat,

Transjordan	trans-jor'duhn
Trans-jordan	trans'jor'duhn
tribunal	tri-by*oo*'nuhl
tribune	trib'y*oo*n
trigon	tr*i*'gon
Tripolis	trip'uh-lis
Troas	troh'az
Trogyllium	troh-jil'ee-uhm
Trophimus	trof'uh-muhs
Tryphaena	tr*i*-fee'nuh
Tryphena	tr*i*-fee'nuh
Trypho	tr*i*'foh
Tryphosa	tr*i*-foh'suh
Tubal	t*oo*'buhl
Tubalcain	t*oo*'buhl-kayn'
Tubal-cain	t*oo*'buhl-kayn'
Tubieni	t*oo*'bee-ee'nee
Twin Brothers	twin'bruh'thuhrz
Tychicus	tik'uh-kuhs
Tyrannus	t*i*-ran'uhs
Tyre	t*i*r
Tyrian	tihr'ee-uhn
Tyrus	t*i*'ruhs
tzaddi	tsahd'ee

U

Ucal	y*oo*'kuhl
Uel	y*oo*'uhl
Uknaz	uhk'naz
Ulai	y*oo*'l*i*
Ulam	y*oo*'luhm
Ulla	uhl'uh
Ummah	uhm'uh
unction	uhnk'shuhn
Unleavened Bread	uhn-lev'uhnd-bred'
Unni	uhn'*i*
Unno	uhn'oh
upharsin	y*oo*-fahr'sin
Uphaz	y*oo*'faz
Ur	oor

---

n **not**, ng **sing**, o **hot**, oh **go**, oi **boy**, oo **foot**, *oo* **boot**, oor **poor**, or **for**,
ou **how**, p **pat**, r **run**, s **so**, sh **sure**, t **toe**, th **thin**, *th* **then**, ts **tsetse**,
tw **twin**, uh **ago**, uhr **her**, v **vow**, w **weather**, y **young**, z **zone**, zh **vision**

Urbane	uhr'bayn
Urbanus	uhr-bay'nuhs
Uri	yoor'*i*
Uriah	yoo-r*i*'uh
Urias	yoo-r*i*'uhs
Uriel	yoor'ee-uhl
Urijah	yoo-r*i*'juh
Urim	yoor'im
Urukian	yoo-rook'ee-uhn
Uthai	y*oo*'th*i*
Uz	uhz
Uzai	y*oo*'z*i*
Uzal	y*oo*'zuhl
Uzza	uhz'uh
Uzzah	uhz'uh
Uzzensheerah	uhz'uhn-shee'uh-ruh
Uzzen-sheerah	uhz'uhn-shee'uh-ruh
Uzzen Sheerah	uhz'uhn-shee'uh-ruh
Uzzen-sherah	uhz'uhn-shee'ruh
Uzzen Sherah	uhz'uhn-shee'ruh
Uzzi	uhz'*i*
Uzzia	uh-z*i*'uh
Uzziah	uh-z*i*'uh
Uzziel	uhz'ee-uhl
Uzzielite	uhz'ee-uh-l*i*t

V

Vaheb	vay'heb
Vaizatha	v*i*'zuh-thuh
Vajezatha	vuh-jez'uh-thuh
Vaniah	vuh-n*i*'uh
Vashni	vash'n*i*
Vashti	vash't*i*
vau	vou
Vedan	vee'duhn
Vophsi	vof's*i*

---

a cat, ah father, ahr lard, air care, aw jaw, ay pay, b bug, ch chew, d do,
e, eh pet, ee seem, er error, f fun, g good, h hot, hw whether, i it, *i* sky,
ihr ear, j joke, k king, kh ch as in German *Buch*, ks vex, kw quill, l love, m mat,

W

Wadi	wah'dee
Waheb	way'heb
waw	wou
Wayiqra	wah-yik'ruh
Weeks	weeks
wen	wen
Whitsuntide	whit'suhn-t*i*d'
Wisdom	wiz'duhm
Wisdom of Jesus ben-Sira	wiz'duhm-uhv-jee'zuhs-ben-s*i*'ruh
Wisdom of Jesus ben Sirach	wiz'duhm-uhv-jee'zuhs-ben-s*i*'ruhk
Wisdom of Jesus the Son of Sirach	wiz'duhm-uhv-jee'suhs-thuh-suhn-uhv-s*i*'ruhk
Wisdom of Sirach	wiz'duhm-uhv-s*i*'ruhk
Wisdom of Solomon	wiz'duhm-uhv-sol'uh-muhn

X

Xanthicus	zan'thi-kuhs
Xerxes	zuhrk'seez

Y

Yad-abshalom	yahd-ab'shuh-luhm
Yah	yah
Yahweh	yah'weh
Yahweh-nissi	yah'weh-nis'*i*
Yahweh-shalom	yah'weh-shah-lohm'
Yahweh-yireh	yah'weh-yihr'ee
Yaudi	yaw'd*i*
Yavan	yay'vuhn
Yehezqel	yuh-hez'kuhl
Yehoshua	yuh-hosh'y*oo*-uh
Yeshayahu	ye'shah-yah'h*oo*

---

n **n**ot, ng si**ng**, o h**o**t, oh g**o**, oi b**oy**, oo f**oo**t, *oo* b**oo**t, oor p**oor**, or f**or**,
ou h**ow**, p **p**at, r **r**un, s **s**o, sh **s**ure, t **t**oe, th **th**in, *th* **th**en, ts **ts**etse,
tw **tw**in, uh **a**go, uhr h**er**, v **v**ow, w **w**eather, y **y**oung, z **z**one, zh vi**s**ion

Yirmeyahu	yihr′muh-yah′h*oo*
Yiron	yihr′uhn
yodh	yohd

Z

Zaanaim	zay′uh-nay′im
Zaanan	zay′uh-nan
Zaanannim	zay′uh-na′nim
Zaavan	zay′uh-vuhn
Zabad	zay′bad
Zabadaius	zab′uh-day′yuhs
Zabadean	zab′uh-dee′uhn
Zabbai	zab′*i*
Zabbud	zab′uhd
Zabdeus	zab′dee-uhs
Zabdi	zab′d*i*
Zabdiel	zab′dee-uhl
Zabud	zay′buhd
Zabulon	zab′yuh-luhn
Zaccai	zak′*i*
Zacchaeus	za-kee′uhs
Zaccheus	za-kee′uhs
Zacchur	zak′uhr
Zaccur	zak′uhr
Zachai	zak′*i*
Zachariah	zak′uh-r*i*′uh
Zacharias	zak′uh-r*i*′uhs
Zacher	zay′kuhr
Zadok	zay′dok
Zadokite	zay′duh-k*i*t
Zaham	zay′ham
Zahar	zay′hahr
zain	zah′yin
Zair	zay′uhr
Zakkur	zak′uhr
Zalaph	zay′laf
Zalmon	zal′muhn
Zalmonah	zal-moh′nuh
Zalmunna	zal-muhn′uh
Zambri	zam′br*i*

---

a cat, ah father, ahr lard, air care, aw jaw, ay pay, b bug, ch chew, d do,
e, eh pet, ee seem, er error, f fun, g good, h hot, hw whether, i it, *i* sky,
ihr ear, j joke, k king, kh ch as in German Buch, ks vex, kw quill, l love, m mat,

Zamoth	zay'moth
Zamzummim	zam-zuh'mim
Zamzummin	zam-zuh'min
Zamzummite	zam-zuh'm*i*t
Zannanim	zuh-na'nim
Zanoah	zuh-noh'uh
Zaphaniah	zaf'uh-n*i*'uh
Zaphenathpaneah	zaf'uh-nath-puh-nee'uh
Zaphenath-paneah	zaf'uh-nath-puh-nee'uh
Zaphnath-paaneah	zaf'nath-pay-uh-nee'uh
Zaphon	zay'fon
Zara	zair'uh
Zaraces	zair'uh-seez
Zarah	zair'uh
Zaraias	zuh-ray'yuhs
Zareah	zair'ee-uh
Zareathite	zair'ee-uh-th*i*t
Zared	zay'rid
Zarephath	zair'uh-fath
Zaretan	zair'uh-tan
Zarethan	zair'uh-than
Zareth-shahar	zair'ith-shay'hahr
Zarhite	zahr'h*i*t
Zarius	zair'ee-uhs
Zartanah	zahr'tuh-nuh
Zarthan	zahr'than
Zathoe	zath'oh-ee
Zathui	zath'*oo*-ee
Zatthu	zat'th*oo*
Zattu	zat'*oo*
Zavan	zay'vuhn
zayin	zah'yin
Zaza	zay'zuh
Zealot	zel'uht
Zebadiah	zeb'uh-d*i*'uh
Zebah	zee'buh
Zebaim	zuh-bay'im
Zebedee	zeb'uh-dee
Zebidah	zuh-b*i*'duh
Zebina	zuh-b*i*'nuh
Zeboiim	zuh-boi'im
Zeboim	zuh-boh'im
Zebub	zee'buhb
Zebudah	zuh-by*oo*'duh
Zebul	zee'buhl

---

n **n**ot, ng si**ng**, o h**o**t, oh g**o**, oi b**oy**, oo f**oo**t, *oo* b**oo**t, oor p**oor**, or f**or**,
ou h**ow**, p **p**at, r **r**un, s **s**o; sh **s**ure, t **t**oe, th **th**in, *th* **th**en, ts **ts**etse,
tw **tw**in, uh **a**go, uhr h**er**, v **v**ow, w **w**eather, y **y**oung, z **z**one, zh vi**s**ion

Zebulonite	zeb'yuh-luh-n*i*t
Zebulun	zeb'yuh-luhn
Zebulunite	zeb'yuh-luh-n*i*t
Zechariah	zek'uh-r*i*'uh
Zecher	zee'kuhr
Zedad	zee'dad
Zedechias	zed'uh-k*i*'uhs
Zedekiah	zed'uh-k*i*'uh
Zeeb	zee'uhb
Zeker	zee'kuhr
Zela	zee'luh
Zelah	zee'luh
Zelek	zee'lik
Zelophehad	zuh-loh'fuh-had
Zelotes	zuh-loh'teez
Zelzah	zel'zuh
Zemaraim	zem'uh-ray'im
Zemarite	zem'uh-r*i*t
Zemer	zee'muhr
Zemira	zuh-m*i*'ruh
Zemirah	zuh-m*i*'ruh
Zenan	zee'nuhn
Zenas	zee'nuhs
Zephaniah	zef'uh-n*i*'uh
Zephath	zee'fath
Zephathah	zef'uh-thuh
Zephi	zee'f*i*
Zepho	zee'foh
Zephon	zee'fon
Zephonite	zee'fuh-n*i*t
Zer	zuhr
Zerah	zihr'uh
Zerahiah	zer'uh-h*i*'uh
Zerahite	zihr'uh-h*i*t
Zeraiah	zuh-ray'yuh
Zerdaiah	zuhr-day'yuh
Zered	zihr'id
Zereda	zer'uh-duh
Zeredah	zer'uh-duh
Zeredatha	zer'uh-day'thuh
Zererah	zer'uh-ruh
Zererath	zer'uh-rath
Zeresh	zihr'ish
Zereth	zihr'ith
Zerethshahar	zihr'ith-shay'hahr

---

a cat, ah father, ahr lard, air care, aw jaw, ay pay, b bug, ch chew, d do,
e, eh pet, ee seem, er error, f fun, g good, h hot, hw whether, i it, *i* sky,
ihr ear, j joke, k king, kh ch as in German Buch, ks vex, kw quill, l love, m mat,

Zereth-shahar	zihr'ith-shay'hahr
Zereth Shahar	zihr'ith-shay'hahr
Zeri	zihr'*i*
Zeror	zihr'or
Zeruah	zuh-r*oo*'uh
Zerubbabel	zuh-ruhb'uh-buhl
Zeruiah	zuh-r*oo*'yuh
Zetham	zee'thuhm
Zethan	zee'thuhn
Zethar	zee'thahr
Zeus	z*oo*s
Zia	z*i*'uh
Ziba	z*i*'buh
Zibeon	zib'ee-uhn
Zibia	zib'ee-uh
Zibiah	zib'ee-uh
Zichri	zik'r*i*
Zicri	zik'r*i*
Ziddim	zid'im
Zidkijah	zid-k*i*'juh
Zidon	z*i*'duhn
Zidonian	z*i*-doh'nee-uhn
Zif	zif
Ziha	z*i*'huh
Ziklag	zik'lag
Zillah	zil'uh
Zillethai	zil'uh-th*i*
Zilpah	zil'puh
Zilthai	zil'th*i*
Zimmah	zim'uh
Zimran	zim'ran
Zimri	zim'r*i*
Zin	zin
Zina	z*i*'nuh
Zion	z*i*'uhn
Zior	z*i*'or
Ziph	zif
Ziphah	z*i*'fuh
Ziphim	zif'im
Ziphion	zif'ee-uhn
Ziphite	zif'*i*t
Ziphron	zif'ron
Zippor	zip'or
Zipporah	z*i*-por'uh
Zithri	zith'r*i*

n not, ng sing, o hot, oh go, oi boy, oo foot, *oo* boot, oor poor, or for,
ou how, p pat, r run, s so, sh sure, t toe, th thin, *th* then, ts tsetse,
tw twin, uh ago, uhr her, v vow, w weather, y young, z zone, zh vision

Ziv	ziv
Ziz	ziz
Ziza	zi″zuh
Zizah	zi″zuh
Zoan	zoh′uhn
Zoar	zoh′ahr
Zoba	zoh′buh
Zobah	zoh′buh
Zobebah	zoh-bee′buh
Zodiac	zoh′dee-ak
Zohar	zoh′hahr
Zoheleth	zoh′huh-lith
Zoheth	zoh′heth
Zophah	zoh′fuh
Zophai	zoh′fi
Zophar	zoh′fahr
Zophim	zoh′fim
Zorah	zor′uh
Zorathite	zor′uh-thit
Zoreah	zoh-ree′uh
Zores	zoh′reez
Zorite	zor′it
Zorobabel	zoh-rob′uh-buhl
Zuar	zoo′uhr
Zuph	zuhf
Zuphite	zoo′fit
Zur	zuhr
Zuriel	zoor′ee-uhl
Zurishaddai	zoor′i-shad′i
Zuth	zooth
Zuzim	zoo′zim
Zuzite	zoo′zit

NONBIBLICAL TERMS

A

Aaronide	air'uh-n*i*d
Ab	ab
Abgarus	ab'guh-ruhs
Accadian	uh-kay'dee-uhn
Acra	ak'ruh
acrostic	uh-kros'tik
Adhonai	ad'oh-n*i*'
Adonis	uh-doh'nis
aeon	ee'uhn
aetiological	ee'tee-uh-loj'i-kuhl
aetiology	ee'tee-ol'uh-jee
agape	ah-gah'pay
Aggadah	uh-gah'duh
aggadic	uh-gah'dik
agora	ag'uh-ruh
agrapha	ag'ruh-fuh
agraphon	ag'ruh-fon
Ahriman	ah'ri-muhn
Ahura-Mazda	uh-hoor'uh-maz'duh
Akhenaton	ahk'uh-nah'tuhn
Akh-en-aton	ahk'uh-nah'tuhn
Akhetaton	ahk'uh-tah'tuhn
Akhnaton	ahk-nah'tuhn
Akiba	uh-kee'buh
Akkadian	uh-kay'dee-uhn
Alexandra	al'ig-zan'druh
Alexandrinus	al'ig-zan-dr*i*'nuhs
Alexandrium	al'ig-zan'dree-uhm
allegorical	al'uh-gor'i-kuhl
allegory	al'uh-gor'ee
Allogenes	a-loj'uh-neez
amanuensis	uh-man'y*oo*-en'sis
Amarna, Tell-el	uh-mahr'nuh, tel'el

Amenhotep	ah'muhn-hoh'tep
'am ha'aretz	ahm'hah-ahr'ets
a minore ad majus	ah-mi-nor'eh-ahd-mah'yoos
'amme ha'aretz	ah'may-hah-ahr'ets
amphictyonic	am-fik'tee-on'ik
amphictyony	am-fik'tee-uh-nee
anacolouthon	an'uh-kuh-loo'thon
anagogic	an'uh-goj'ik
anagogical	an'uh-goj'i-kuhl
anagogy	an'uh-goh'jee
analogical	an'uh-loj'i-kuhl
analogy	uh-nal'uh-jee
anaphora	uh-naf'uh-ruh
Anat	ah'naht
androgynous	an-droj'i-nuhs
androgyny	an-droj'uh-nee
angelology	ayn'juhl-ol'uh-jee
Annunciation	uh-nuhn'see-ay'shuhn
anthropological	an'thruh-puh-loj'i-kuhl
anthropology	an'thruh-pol'uh-jee
anthropomorphic	an'thruh-puh-mor'fik
anthropomorphism	an'thruh-puh-mor'fiz-uhm
Antilibanus	an'ti-lib'uh-nuhs
antinomian	an'ti-noh'mee-uhn
antinomianism	an'ti-noh'mee-uh-niz-uhm
Antitheses	an-tith'uh-seez
Antonia	an'toh'nee-uh
Antonius	an'toh'nee-uhs
aphorism	af'uh-riz'uhm
aphoristic	af'uh-ris'tik
'Apiru	ah'pi-*roo*
apocalyptic	uh-pok'uh-lip'tik
apocalypticism	uh-pok'uh-lip'tuh-siz-uhm
Apocrypha	uh-pok'ruh-fuh
apocryphal	uh-pok'ruh-fuhl
Apocryphon	uh-pok'ruh-fon
apodictic	ap'uh-dik'tik
apodosis	uh-pod'uh-sis
Apollonius	ap'uh-loh'nee-uhs
apologetic	up-pol'uh-jet'ik
apologia	ap'uh-loh-jee'uh
apologist	uh-pol'uh-jist
apology	uh-pol'uh-jee
apophthegm	ap'uhf-them'
Apostolicon	ap'uhs-stol'i-kon

---

a cat, ah father, ahr lard, air care, aw jaw, ay pay, b bug, ch chew, d do,
e, eh pet, ee seem, er error, f fun, g good, h hot, hw whether, i it, *i* sky,
ihr ear, j joke, k king, kh **ch** as in German *Buch*, ks vex, kw quill, l love, m mat,

apothegm	ap'uh-them'
apparatus criticus	ap'uh-rat'uhs-krit'i-kuhs
Aqiba	uh-kee'buh
Arabic	air'uh-bik
Aramaism	air'uh-may-iz-uhm
Aratus	air'uh-tuhs
archon	ahr'kohn
aretalogical	air'uh-tuh-loj'i-kuhl
aretalogy	air'uh-tahl'uh-jee
Aristeas	air'is-tee'uhs
Aristotelian	air'is-tuh-teel'yuhn
Aristotelianism	air'is-tuh-teel'yuhn-iz-uhm
Aristotle	air'is-tot'uhl
Armenian	ahr-mee'nee-uhn
Ascension	uh-sen'shuhn
Asclepius	as-klee'pee-uhs
Ashurnasirpal	ash'uhr-nas'uhr-puhl
Ash Wednesday	ash'wenz'day
asyndeton	uh-sin'duh-ton'
Augustine	aw-gus'tin
Augustinian	aw-gus-tin'ee-uhn
Augustinianism	aw-gus-tin'ee-uhn-iz'uhm
Avaris	uh-vahr'is
Avesta	uh-ves'tuh

B

Baalbek	bay'uhl-bek
Bacchi	bak'i
Bacchus	bak'uhs
bar	bahr
Bar Cochba	bahr-kohk'buh
Bar Cochbah	bahr-kohk'buh
Bar Cocheba	bahr-kohk'uh-buh
Bar Cochebah	bahr-kohk'uh-buh
Bar Cosiba	bahr-koh'si-buh
Bar Cosibah	bahr-koh'si-buh
Bar Coziba	bahr-koh'zi-buh
Bar Cozibah	bahr-koh'zi-buh
Baris	bair'is
Bar Kochba	bahr-kohk'buh

---

n not, ng sing, o hot, oh go, oi boy, oo foot, *oo* boot, oor poor, or for,
ou how, p pat, r run, s so, sh sure, t toe, th thin, *th* then, ts tsetse,
tw twin, uh ago, uhr her, v vow, w weather, y young, z zone, zh vision

Bar Kochbah	bahr-kohk′buh
Bar Kocheba	bahr-kohk′uh-buh
Bar Kochebah	bahr-kohk′uh-buh
Bar Kokhba	bahr-kohk′buh
Bar Kokhbah	bahr-kohk′buh
Bar Kosiba	bahr-koh′si-buh
Bar Kosibah	bahr-koh′si-buh
Bar Koziba	bahr-koh′zi-buh
Bar Kozibah	bahr-koh′zi-buh
Bashmuric	bash-moor′ik
Basilides	bas′i-li′deez
Bath Qol	bath-kohl′
Beatitude	bee-at′uh-tyood
Beatty	bee′tee
bema	bee′muh
benediction	ben′uh-dik′shuhn
Benedictus	ben′uh-dik′toohs
Bezae Cantabrigiensis	bee′zee-kan′tuh-brij-ee-en′sis
bios	bi′os
Bodmer	bod′muhr
Bohairic	boh-hi′rik
Byzantine	biz′uhn-teen

C

Caesarean	ses′uh-ree′uhn
Caligula	kuh-lig′yuh-luh
Cambyses	kam-bi′seez
canon	kan′uhn
canonical	kuh-non′i-kuhl
canonicity	kan′uh-nis′uh-tee
canonization	kan′uh-ni-zay′shuhn
canonize	kan′uh-niz
casuistic	kas′yoo-is′tik
casuistry	kas′yoo-is-tree
catechesis	kat′uh-kee′sis
catechetic	kat′uh-ket′ik
catechetical	kat′uh-ket′i-kuhl
catechism	kat′uh-kiz′uhm
catena	kuh-tee′nuh
Catholic	kath′uh-lik

---

a cat, ah father, ahr lard, air care, aw jaw, ay pay, b bug, ch chew, d do,
e, eh pet, ee seem, er error, f fun, g good, h hot, hw whether, i it, *i* sky,
ihr ear, j joke, k king, kh ch as in German *Buch*, ks vex, kw quill, l love, m mat,

Celsus	sel'suhs
Cerinthus	suh-rin'thuhs
Chabiru	hah-bee'r*oo*
Chalcolithic	kal'kuh-lith'ik
Chanukkah	hah'nuh-kuh
Chapiru	hah-pee'r*oo*
charism	kair'iz'uhm
charisma	kuh-riz'muh
charismata	kuh-riz'muh-tah
charismatic	kair'riz-mat'ik
Chasidic	hah-sid'ik
Chasidim	has'uh-dim
Chenoboskion	ken'aw-bos'kee-uhn
cherem	her'im
chesed	hee'sid
chiasm	k*i*'az'uhm
chiasma	k*i*-az'muh
chiasmus	k*i*-az'muhs
chiastic	k*i*-as'tik
chiliasm	kil'i-az'uhm
chiliast	kil'ee-ast
chiliastic	kil'ee-as'tik
Chosiba	koh'si-buh
Chosibah	koh'si-buh
Choziba	koh'zi-buh
Chozibah	koh'zi-buh
chreia	kray'uh
chria	kree'uh
Christogenesis	kris'toh-jen'uh-sis
christological	krist'uh-loj'i-kuhl
Christology	kris-tol'uh-jee
Christophany	kris-tof'uh-nee
Chronicler	kron'i-kluhr
chronos	kroh'nohs
Cicero	sis'uh-roh
Cimmerian	si'mihr'ee-uhn
Claromantanus	klair'uh-mon-tan'uhs
Clementine	klem'uhn-t*i*n
Cleodemus	klee-oh'duh-muhs
Cochba	kohk'buh
Cochbah	kohk'buh
Cocheba	koh'kuh-buh
Cochebah	koh'kuh-buh
codex	koh'deks
codices	koh'duh-seez

n not, ng sing, o hot, oh go, oi boy, oo foot, *oo* boot, oor poor, or for,
ou how, p pat, r run, s so, sh sure, t toe, th thin, *th* then, ts tsetse,
tw twin, uh ago, uhr her, v vow, w weather, y young, z zone, zh vision

collate	kol′ayt
collation	kol-ay′shuhn
colon	koh′luhn
colophon	kol′uh-fon
Complutensian Polyglot	kom-pl*oo*-ten′see-uhn-pol′ee-glot
concordance	kuhn-kord′uhns
conflate	kuhn-flayt′
conflation	kuhn-flay′shuhn
Copt	kopt
Coptic	kop′tik
Corpus Hermeticum	kor′puhs-huhr-met′i-kuhm
Cosiba	koh′si-buh
Cosibah	koh′si-buh
cosmogony	koz-mog′uh-nee
cosmography	kos-mog′ruh-fee
cosmological	kos′muh-loj′i-kuhl
cosmology	koz-mol′uh-jee
Coziba	koh′zi-buh
Cozibah	koh′zi-buh
Coverdale	kuhv′uhr-dayl
credo	kree′doh
critical apparatus	krit′i-kuhl-ap-uh-rat′uhs
Crucifixion	kr*oo*′suh-fik′shuhn
crucify	kr*oo*′suh-f*i*
cryptogram	krip′tuh-gram
cryptography	krip-tog′ruh-fee
Cuneiform	ky*oo*-nee′uh-form
Curetonian	kyoor′uh-toh′nee-uhn
cursive	kuhr′siv
Cynic	sin′ik
Cynicism	sin′uh-siz′uhm
Cypros	s*i*′pros

D

Davidic	duh-vid′ik
decalogue	dek′uh-log
Decapolis	di-kap′uh-lis
Demeter	di-mee′tuhr
Demiurge	dem′ee-uhrj
demonology	dee′muhn-ol′uh-jee

---

a cat, ah father, ahr lard, air care, aw jaw, ay pay, b bug, ch chew, d do,
e, eh pet, ee seem, er error, f fun, g good, h hot, hw whether, i it, *i* sky,
ihr ear, j joke, k king, kh ch as in German *Buch*, ks vex, kw quill, l love, m mat,

demythologization	dee′mith-ol′uh-j*i*-zay′shuhn
demythologize	dee′mith-ol′uh-j*i*z
demythologizing	dee′mith-ol′uh-j*i*z-ing
Deuter*o*canon	dy*oo*′tuh-roh-kan′uhn
deuterocanonical	dy*oo*′tuh-roh-kuh-non′i-kuhl
deuterograph	dy*oo*′tuh-roh-graf′
deuterographic	dy*oo*′tuh-roh-graf′ik
Deutero-Isaiah	dy*oo*′tuh-roh-*i*-zay′yuh
Deuteronomic	dy*oo*′tuh-ruh-nom′ik
Deuteronomist	dy*oo*′tuh-ron′uh-mist
Deuteronomistic	dy*oo*′tuh-ron′uh-mis′tik
Deutero-Pauline	dy*oo*′tuh-roh-paw′l*i*n
diachronic	d*i*′uh-kron′ik
Diatessaron	d*i*′uh-tes′uh-ron
diatribe	d*i*′uh-tr*i*b′
Didache	did′uh-kee
didrachma	d*i*-drak′muh
Didyma	did′uh-muh
Diognetus	d*i*-og′ni-tuhs
Dionysia	d*i*′uh-nish′ee-uh
Dismas	diz′muhs
dittography	di-tog′ruh-fee
Dives	d*i*′veez
docetic	doh-set′ik
Docetism	doh′suh-tiz′uhm
dolmen	dol′muhn
dominical	duh-min′uh-kuhl
Domitian	duh-mish′uhn
Douay	d*oo*′ay
doxology	dok-sol′uh-jee
Dura-Europus	door′uh-yoor-oh′puhs
Dysmas	diz′muhs

E

Ebionite	ee′bee-uh-n*i*t
Ebla	eb′luh
Ecce Homo	ek′eh-hoh′moh
ecclesia	i-klee′zhee-uh
ecclesial	i-klee′zee-uhl
ecclesiastic	i-klee′zee-as′tik

n **not**, ng **sing**, o **hot**, oh **go**, oi **boy**, oo **foot**, *oo* **boot**, oor **poor**, or **for**,
ou **how**, p **pat**, r **run**, s **so**, sh **sure**, t **toe**, th **thin**, *th* **then**, ts **tsetse**,
tw **twin**, uh **ago**, uhr **her**, v **vow**, w **weather**, y **young**, z **zone**, zh **vision**

ecclesiastical	i-klee′zee-as′ti-kuhl
ecclesiological	i-klee′zee-uh-loj′i-kuhl
ecclesiology	i-klee′zee-ol′uh-jee
ecstasy	ek′stuh-see
ecstatic	ek-stat′ik
ecumenical	ek′yoo-men′i-kuhl
Egnatian	eg′nay′shuhn
eisegesis	*is*′uh-jee′suhs
eisegetical	*is*′uh-jet′i-kuhl
ekklesia	i-klee′zhee-uh
Elephantine	el′uh-fan-t*i*′nee
Eleusinian	el′y*oo*-sin′ee-uhn
Eleusis	i-*loo*′sis
Elohim	el′oh-him
Elohist	el′oh-hist
El Shaddai	el-shad′*i*
El Shadday	el-shad′*i*
Elyon	el-yohn′
Encratite	en′kruh-t*i*t
Encratitic	en′kruh-t*i*′tik
Endzeit	ent′ts*i*t
Enlil	en′lil
Enuma Elish	en-*oo*′muh-el′ish
Ephraemi Rescriptus	ee′fruh-mee-ri-skrip′tuhs
Epictetus	ep′ik-tee′tuhs
Epicurean	ep′uh-kyoo-ree′uhn
Epicureanism	ep′uh-kyoo-ree′uhn-iz-uhm
Epicurus	ep′uh-kyoor′uhs
epiphany	i-pif′uh-nee
episcopacy	i-pis′kuh-puh-see
episcopal	i-pis′kuh-puhl
episcopate	i-pis′kuh-payt
eponym	ep′uh-nim
eponymic	ep′uh-nim′ik
eponymous	i-pon′uh-muhs
eponymy	i-pon′uh-mee
eschatological	es′kat-uh-loj′i-kuhl
eschatology	es′kuh-tol′uh-jee
eschaton	es′kuh-ton
Essene	es′een
Ethiopic	ee′thee-op′ik
etiological	ee′tee-uh-loj′i-kuhl
etiology	ee′tee-ol′uh-jee
etymological	et′uh-muh-loj′i-kuhl
etymology	et′uh-mol′uh-jee

a cat, ah father, ahr lard, air care, aw jaw, ay pay, b bug, ch chew, d do,
e, eh pet, ee seem, er error, f fun, g good, h hot, hw whether, i it, *i* sky,
ihr ear, j joke, k king, kh ch as in German Buch, ks vex, kw quill, l love, m mat,

Eucharist	yoo′kuh-rist
eucharistic	yoo′kuh-ris′tik
Eugnostos	yoog-nos′tuhs
Eusebius	yoo-see′bee-uhs
Eusebius Pamphili	yoo-see′bee-uhs-pam′fil-ee
Evangelistarion	i-vahn′juh-lis-tair′ee-on
Evangelium	i-van-jel′ee-uhm
Evodius	i-voh′dee-uhs
exegesis	ek′suh-jee′suhs
exegete	ek′suh-jeet
exegetical	ek′suh-jet′i-kuhl
existential	eg′zi-sten′shuhl
existentialism	eg′zi-sten′shuhl-iz′uhm
existentialist	eg′zi-sten′shuhl-ist
exorcise	ek′sor-*siz*
exorcism	ek′sor-siz′uhm
exorcist	ek′sor-sist
exorcize	ek′sor-*siz*
exposition	ek′spuh-zish′uhn
expository	ek-spos′uh-tor′ee

F

Flavius	flay′vee-uhs
Florilegium	flor′uh-leej′ee-uhm
Formgeschichte	form′ge-shikh′teh
Forschung	for′shoonk
Fruehkatholizismus	free′kah-tohl′i-tsis′muhs

G

Gaius	gay′uhs
Gattung	gah′toonk
Gattungen	gah′toong-en
Gattungsforschung	gah′toonks-for′shoong
Gattungsgeschichte	gah′toonks-ge-shikh′teh
Gemara	guh-mah′ruh

---

n **not**, ng **sing**, o **hot**, oh **go**, oi **boy**, oo **foot**, *oo* **boot**, oor **poor**, or **for**,
ou **how**, p **pat**, r **run**, s **so**, sh **sure**, t **toe**, th **thin**, *th* **then**, ts **tsetse**,
tw **twin**, uh **ago**, uhr **her**, v **vow**, w **weather**, y **young**, z **zone**, zh **vision**

Gemeindeordnung	ge-m*i*n'deh-ord'noonk
Gemeindeordnungen	ge-m*i*n'deh-ord'noong-en
Gemeinderegel	ge-m*i*n'deh-ray'gel
Gemeinderegeln	ge-m*i*n'deh-ray'geln
genealogical	jee'nee-uh-loj'i-kuhl
genealogy	jee'nee-al'uh-jee
genizah	guh-neet'suh
genre	zhahn'ruh
ger	guhr
Geschichte	ge-shikh'teh
geschichtlich	ge-shikht'likh
Gilgamesh	gil'guh-mesh
glossalalia	glos'uh-lay'lee-uh
gnosis	noh'sis
Gnostic	nos'tik
Gnosticism	nos'tuh-siz'uhm
Griesbach	grees'bahkh
Grundlage	groont'lah-geh

H

Habiru	hah-bee'r*oo*
Hadrian	hay'dree-uhn
Haggadah	huh-gah'duh
haggadic	huh-gah'dik
Hagiographa	hag'ee-og'ruh-fuh
hagiographon	hag'ee-og'ruh-fon
Halachah	hah'lah-kah'
halachic	hah-lah'kik
Halakah	hah'lah-kah'
halakic	hah-lah'kik
Hammurabi	ham'uh-rah'bee
Hammurapi	ham'uh-rah'pee
Hanukkah	hah'nuh-kuh
hapax	hah'pahks
hapax legomena	hah'pahks-luh-gohm'uh-nuh
hapax legomenon	hah'pahks-luh-gohm'uh-non
Hapiru	hah-pee'r*oo*
haplography	hap-log'ruh-fee
Hasid	hah'sid
Hasidic	hah-sid'ik

---

a cat, ah father, ahr lard, air care, aw jaw, ay pay, b bug, ch chew, d do,
e, eh pet, ee seem, er error, f fun, g good, h hot, hw whether, i it, *i* sky,
ihr ear, j joke, k king, kh ch as in German Buch, ks vex, kw quill, l love, m mat,

Hasidim	has'uh-dim
Hasmonaean	haz'muh-nee'uhn
Hasmonean	haz'muh-nee'uhn
Hattin	hah-teen'
Haustafel	hous'tah-fel
Haustafeln	hous'tah-feln
Heilsgeschichte	h*i*ls'ge-shikh'teh
heilsgeschichtlich	h*i*ls'ge-shikht'likh
hellenize	hel'uh-n*i*z'
hendiadys	hen-d*i*'uh-duhs
henotheism	hen'uh-thee-iz'uhm
henotheist	hen'uh-thee-ist
henotheistic	hen-uh-thee-is'tik
Heptateuch	hep'tuh-ty*oo*k
herem	her'im
hermeneut	huhr'muh-ny*oo*t
hermeneutic	huhr'muh-ny*oo*'tik
hermeneutical	huhr'muh-ny*oo*'ti-kuhl
Hermetic	huhr-met'ik
Hermeticum, Corpus	huhr-met'i-kuhm, kor'puhs
Herodium	hi-roh'dee-uhm
hesed	hee'sid
hexapla	hek'suh-pluh
Hexateuch	hek'suh-ty*oo*k
hierocracy	h*i*'uh-rok'ruh-see
hieroglyph	h*i*'ruh-glif
hieroglyphic	h*i*'ruh-glif'ik
hieros logos	h*i*'uh-rohs-loh'gohs
Historie	his'toh-ree'
historisch	his-toh'rish
homiletic	hom'uh-let'ik
homily	hom'uh-lee
homoioteleuton	hoh-moi'oh-tel'y*oo*-ton
Hurrian	hoor'ee-uhn
Hyksos	hik'sohs
hypotactic	h*i*'puh-tak'tik
hypotaxis	h*i*'puh-tak'sis
Hyrcania	huhr-kay'nee-uh

---

n **not**, ng **sing**, o **hot**, oh **go**, oi **boy**, oo **foot**, *oo* **boot**, oor **poor**, or **for**,
ou **how**, p **pat**, r **run**, s **so**, sh **sure**, t **toe**, th **thin**, *th* **then**, ts **tsetse**,
tw **twin**, uh **ago**, uhr **her**, v **vow**, w **weather**, y **young**, z **zone**, zh **vision**

I

icon	*i*′kon
iconoclasm	*i*-kon′uh-klaz′uhm
iconoclastic	*i*-kon′uh-klas′tik
iconography	*i*′kuh-nog′ruh-fee
Ignatius	ig-nay′shuhs
Ikhnaton	ik-nah′tuhn
Incarnation	in′kahr-nay′shuhn
inclusio	in-kl*oo*′zhee-oh
inerrancy	in-er′uhn-see
inerrant	in-er′uhnt
interpolate	in-tuhr′puh-layt′
interpolation	in-tuhr′puh-lay′shuhn
iotacism	*i*-oh′tuh-siz′uhm
ipsissima verba	ip-sis′i-muh-wer′bah
ipsissima vox	ip-sis′i-muh-woks
ipsissimum verbum	ip-sis′i-moom-wer′boom
Iran	i-ran′
Irenaeus	*i*′ruh-nee′uhs
Ishtar	ish′tahr
Isis	*i*′sis
itacism	it′uh-siz′uhm

J

Jahveh	yah′weh
Jahvist	yah′wist
Jahweh	yah′weh
Jahwist	yah′wist
Janneus	ja-nee′uhs
Jaulan	jaw′luhn
Jehovah-shamma	ji-hoh′vuh-sham′uh
Jehovah-tsidkenu	ji-hoh′vuh-tsid-ken′*oo*
Jerash	jer′ash
Jerome	juh-rohm′
Johannine	joh-han′*i*n
Judaeus	j*oo*-dee′uhs
Judaic	j*oo*-day′ik

---

a cat, ah father, ahr lard, air care, aw jaw, ay pay, b bug, ch chew, d do,
e, eh pet, ee seem, er error, f fun, g good, h hot, hw whether, i it, *i* sky,
ihr ear, j joke, k king, kh ch as in German Buch, ks vex, kw quill, l love, m mat,

Judaize	joo'day-iz
Judaizer	joo'day-iz'uhr
Judaizing	joo'day-iz'ing
Judeus	joo-dee'uhs
Jung	yoong
Justin Martyr	juhs'tin-mahr'tuhr

K

Kaddish	kah'dish
kairos	ki'rohs
Kenoboskion	ken'aw-bos'kee-uhn
kenosis	ki-noh'sis
kenotic	ki-not'ik
Kerak	kuhr'ahk
kere	kuh-ray'
kerygma	ki-rig'muh
kerygmatic	ker'ig-mat'ik
kesitah	kes'i-tah
Kethibh	kuh-theev'
Kethubhim	ki-thoo'vim
Ketubim	ki-thoo'bim
Kethuvim	ki-thoo'vim
Ketubhim	ki-too'vim
Ketubim	ki-too'bim
Ketuvim	ki-too'vim
Khapiru	hah-pee'roo
Khirbet	kihr'bet
Kibbroth-hattavah	kib'roth-haht'ah-vah
Kochba	kohk'buh
Kochbah	kohk'buh
Kocheba	koh'kuh-buh
Kochebah	koh'kuh-buh
Koine	koi-nay'
Kokhba	kohk'buh
Kokhbah	kohk'buh
Kokheba	koh'kuh-buh
Kokhebah	koh'kuh-buh
Kompositionsgeschichte	kom'poh-zit-see-ohns'ge-shikh'teh
kompositionsgeschichtlich	kom'poh-zit-see-ohns'ge-shikht'likh
kosher	koh'shuhr

n not, ng sing, o hot, oh go, oi boy, oo foot, *oo* boot, oor poor, or for,
ou how, p pat, r run, s so, sh sure, t toe, th thin, *th* then, ts tsetse,
tw twin, uh ago, uhr her, v vow, w weather, y young, z zone, zh vision

Kosiba	koh'si-buh
Kosibah	koh'si-buh
Koziba	koh'zi-buh
Kozibah	koh'zi-buh
Kultgeschichte	koolt'ge-shikh'teh
kultgeschichtlich	koolt'ge-shikht'likh
Kultgeschichtliche Schule	koolt'ge-shikht'likh-eh-shool'eh
Kunstprosa	koonst'proh-sah
Kunstspruch	koonst'shprookh
kyrios	kihr'ee-ohs

L

lacuna	luh-ky*oo*'nuh
lacunae	luh-ky*oo*'nee
Latinism	lat'uh-niz'uhm
Leben Jesu Forschung	lay'ben-yay's*oo*-for'shoong
lectio difficilior probabilior	lek'tee-oh-dif-i-kil'ee-or-proh-buh-bil'ee-or
lectionary	lek'shuh-ner'ee
Lentulus	len'chuh-luhs
Lesbos	lez'buhs
Leucius	l*oo*'shee-uhs
Levant	luh-vant'
Levantine	lev'uhn-teen
Levirate	lev'uh-rit
lexical	lek'si-kuhl
lexicography	lek'si-kog'ruh-fee
lexicon	lek'si-kon
lex talionis	leks'tal-ee-oh'nis
liturgical	li-tuhr'ji-kuhl
liturgy	lit'uhr-jee
locus classicus	loh'koohs-klahs'i-koohs
logia	loh'jee-ah
logion	loh'jee-on
Logos	loh'gohs

---

a cat, ah father, ahr lard, air care, aw jaw, ay pay, b bug, ch chew, d do,
e, eh pet, ee seem, er error, f fun, g good, h hot, hw whether, i it, *i* sky,
ihr ear, j joke, k king, kh ch as in German *Buch*, ks vex, kw quill, l love, m mat,

M

Machaerus	muh-kihr'uhs
Madeba	mad'uh-buh
Magnesian	mag-nee'zhuhn
Magnificat	mag-nif'uh-kat
Mandaean	man-dee'uhn
Mandaeism	man-dee'iz-uhm
Mandean	man-dee'uhn
Mandeism	man-dee'iz-uhm
Manes	may'neez
Mani	mah'nee
Manichaean	man'uh-kee'uhn
Manichaeism	man'uh-kee-iz'uhm
Manichean	man'uh-kee'uhn
Manicheism	man'uh-kee-iz'uhm
Manicheus	man'uh-kee'uhs
Marcion	mahr'shuhn
Marcionism	mahr'shuh-niz'uhm
Marcionite	mahr'shuh-n*i*t
Marcionitism	mahr'shuh-n*i*t-iz'uhm
Mari	mah'ree
Martyr	mahr'tuhr
martyrdom	mahr'tuhr-duhm
Masada	muh-sah'duh
Masora	muh-sor'uh
Masorah	muh-sor'uh
Masorete	mas'uh-reet
Masoretic	mas'uh-ret'ik
Massada	muh-sah'duh
Massebah	mas'uh-buh
Massorah	muh-sor'uh
Massorete	mas'uh-reet
Massoretic	mas'uh-ret'ik
Maundy	mawn'dee
Megillah	mi-gil'uh
Megillot	mi-gil'ot
Megilloth	mi-gil'oth
Melchior	mel'kee-or
Melito	mel'i-toh
Melkon	mel'kon
Menander	muh-nan'duhr
menorah	muh-nor'uh
Merenptah	muhr'enp-tah'

n **n**ot, ng si**ng**, o h**o**t, oh g**o**, oi b**oy**, oo f**oo**t, *oo* b**oo**t, oor p**oor**, or f**or**, ou h**ow**, p **p**at, r **r**un, s **s**o, sh **s**ure, t **t**oe, th **th**in, *th* **th**en, ts **ts**etse, tw **tw**in, uh **a**go, uhr h**er**, v **v**ow, w **w**eather, y **y**oung, z **z**one, zh vi**s**ion

Merneptah	muhr'nep-tah'
Mer-ne-ptah	muhr'nep-tah'
messiahship	muh-s*i*'uh-ship
Messianic	mes'ee-an'ik
messianism	mes'ee-uhn-iz'uhm
metonymy	muh-ton'uh-mee
mezuzah	muh-z*oo*'zuh
midrashim	mid-rash'im
migdal	mig'duhl
millenarian	mil'uh-nair'ee-uhn
millenarianism	mil'uh-nair'ee-uhn-iz'uhm
millennial	muh-len'ee-uhl
millennialism	muh-len'ee-uhl-iz'uhm
millennialist	muh-len'ee-uhl-ist
Millennium	muh-len'ee-uhm
Minaean	min-ee'uhn
minuscule	min'uh-sky*oo*l
Mishna	mish'nuh
Mishnah	mish'nuh
Mitanni	mi-tan'ee
Mithra	mith'ruh
Mithraic	mith-ray'ik
Mithraism	mith'ruh-iz'uhm
Mithras	mith'ruhs
monolatrous	muh-nol'uh-truhs
monolatry	muh-nol'uh-tree
monotheism	mon'uh-thee-iz'uhm
monotheist	mon'uh-thee-ist
monotheistic	mon-uh-thee-is'tik
Montanism	mon'tuh-niz'uhm
Montanus	mon'tuh-nuhs
Mosaic	moh-zay'ik
Muratorian	myoor'uh-tor'ee-uhn

N

Nabataea	nab'uh-tee'uh
Nabataean	nab'uh-tee'uhn
Nabatea	nab'uh-tee'uh
nabhi	nah-vee'
nabi	nah-bee'

a cat, ah father, ahr lard, air care, aw jaw, ay pay, b bug, ch chew, d do,
e, eh pet, ee seem, er error, f fun, g good, h hot, hw whether, i it, *i* sky,
ihr ear, j joke, k king, kh ch as in German *Buch*, ks vex, kw quill, l love, m mat,

Nablus	nab'luhs
Nabonidus	nab'uh-ni'duhs
Nabopolassar	nab'uh-puh-las'uhr
Nag Hammadi	nahg'huh-mah'dee
Nash	nash
navi	nah-vee'
nebhiim	nuh-vee'im
nebiim	nuh-bee'im
necromancy	nek'ruh-man'see
Neolithic	nee'uh-lith'ik
Neriglissar	nuhr'ig-lis'uhr
neviim	nuh-vee'im
Nimrud	nim'rood
Nippur	ni-poor'
Novelle	noh-wel'eh
Nunc Dimittis	noonk'di-mit'is
Nuzi	noo'zee

O

obelisk	ob'uh-lisk
Ode	ohd
onomastica	on'uh-mas'tuh-kuh
onomasticon	on'uh-mas'tuh-kon
oracle	or'uh-kuhl
oracular	or-ak'yuh-luhr
Origen	or'uh-juhn
Orontes	or-on'teez
Orphica	or'fuh-kuh
orthodox	or'thuh-doks
orthodoxy	or'thuh-dok'see
Osiris	oh-si'ruhs
ossuary	os'yoo-er'ee
Ostia	os'tee-uh
ostraca	os'truh-kuh
ostracon	os'truh-kon
Oxyrhyncus	ok'si-ring'kuhs

---

n not, ng sing, o hot, oh go, oi boy, oo foot, *oo* boot, oor poor, or for,
ou how, p pat, r run, s so, sh sure, t toe, th thin, *th* then, ts tsetse,
tw twin, uh ago, uhr her, v vow, w weather, y young, z zone, zh vision

P

paleography	pay'lee-og'ruh-fee
Paleolithic	pay'lee-uh-lith'ik
palimpsest	pal'imp-sest
Papias	pay'pee-uhs
papyri	puh-p*i*'r*i*
papyrus	puh-p*i*'ruhs
paradigm	pair'uh-d*i*m
paradigmatic	pair'uh-dig-mat'ik
paraenesis	pair'uh-nee'sis
paraenetic	pair'uh-net'ik
parallelism	pair'uh-lel-iz'uhm
paratactic	pair'uh-tak'tik
parataxis	pair'uh-tak'sis
parchment	pahrch'muhnt
parenesis	pair'uh-nee'sis
parenetic	pair'uh-net'ik
paronomasia	pair'uh-noh-may'zhee-uh
Parousia	puh-r*oo*'zhee-uh
Passion	pash'uhn
Pastoral	pas'tuhr-uhl
patriarch	pay'tree-ahrk
patriarchal	pay'tree-ahr'kuhl
patristic	puh-tris'tik
Pauline	paw'l*i*n
Pella	pel'uh
Pentateuch	pen'tuh-ty*oo*k
Peraea	puh-ree'uh
Perea	puh-ree'uh
pericopae	puh-rik'uh-pee
pericope	puh-rik'uh-pee
pesher	pesh'uhr
pesherim	pesh'uh-rim
Peshitta	puh-shee'tuh
Petra	pee'truh
Petrine	pee'tr*i*n
Phasael	fah'see-uhl
Phasaelis	fuh-see'luhs
Phasaelus	fuh-see'luhs
Philadelphian	fil'uh-del'fee-uhn
Philo	f*i*'loh
phylactery	fi'lak'tuh-ree
Plato	play'toh

a cat, ah father, ahr lard, air care, aw jaw, ay pay, b bug, ch chew, d do,
e, eh pet, ee seem, er error, f fun, g good, h hot, hw whether, i it, *i* sky,
ihr ear, j joke, k king, kh ch as in German *Buch*, ks vex, kw quill, l love, m mat,

Platonic	pluh-ton'ik
Platonism	play'tuh-niz'uhm
pleonasm	plee'uh-naz'uhm
pleonastic	plee'uh-nas'tik
pleroma	pli-roh'muh
Pliny	plin'ee
Plutarch	ploo'tahrk
pneuma	nyoo'muh
pneumatic	nyoo-mat'ik
pneumatology	nyoo'muh-tol'uh-jee
polis	poh'lis
Polycarp	pol'ee-kahrp
Polyglot	pol'ee-glot
Polyglot, Complutensian	pol'ee-glot, kom-ploo-ten'see-uhn
polytheism	pol'ee-thee-iz'uhm
polytheistic	pol'ee-thee-is'tik
polyvalence	pol'ee-vay'luhns
polyvalent	pol'ee-vay'luhnt
Pompey	pom'pee
praetor	pree'tuhr
pretor	pree'tuhr
prolepsis	proh-lep'sis
proleptic	proh-lep'tik
protasis	prot'uh-sis
Protennoia	proh'tuh-noi'yuh
Protevangelium	proh'ti-van-jel'ee-uhm
Protoevangelium	proh'toh-i-van-jel'ee-uhm
Proto-Luke	proh'toh-look'
Proto-Matthew	proh'toh-math'yoo
psalmody	sah'muh-dee
Psalter	sawl'tuhr
Pseudepigrapha	soo'duh-pig'ruh-fuh
pseudepigraphal	soo'duh-pig'ruh-fuhl
pseudepigraphical	sood'ep-i-graf'i-kuhl
pseudepigraphon	soo'duh-pig'ruh-fon
pseudepigraphy	soo'duh-pig'ruh-fee
pseudo	soo'doh
Pseudo-Eupolemus	soo'doh-yoo-pol'uh-muhs
Pseudo-Hecataeus	soo'doh-hek'uh-tee'uhs
Pseudo-Jonathan	soo'doh-jon'uh-thuhn
Pseudo-Matthew	soo'doh-math'yoo
Pseudo-Melito	soo'doh-mel'i-toh
pseudonym	soo'duh-nim
pseudonymity	soo'duh-nim'uh-tee
pseudonymous	soo-don'uh-muhs

n not, ng sing, o hot, oh go, oi boy, oo foot, *oo* boot, oor poor, or for,
ou how, p pat, r run, s so, sh sure, t toe, th thin, *th* then, ts tsetse,
tw twin, uh ago, uhr her, v vow, w weather, y young, z zone, zh vision

Pseudo-Philo	*soo*'doh-fi'loh
Pseudo-Phocylides	*soo*'doh-foh-sil'uh-deez
Ptolemaic	tol'uh-may'ik

Q

Qarqar	kahr'kahr
Qere	kuh-ray'
Qere-Kethibh	kuh-ray'kuh-theev'
qesita	kes'i-tah
Quadratus	kwahd'ruh-tuhs
Quelle	kvel'eh
Quellenkritik	kvel'en-kri-teek'
Qumran	koom'rahn
Qurun Hattin	koo'roon-hah-teen'

R

Ra	rah
rabbinic	ruh-bin'ik
rabbinism	rab'in-iz'uhm
Ramesses	ram'uh-seez
Ramses	ram'seez
Ras-shamra	rahs-shahm'ruh
Ras Shamra	rahs-shahm'ruh
Re	ray
recension	ri-sen'shuhn
redact	ri-dakt'
redaction	ri-dak'shuhn
redactional	ri-dak'shuhn-uhl
radactor	ri-dak'tuhr
Redaktionsgeschichte	ray-dahk'tee-ohns'ge-shikh'teh
redaktionsgeschichtlich	ray-dahk'tee-ohns'ge-shikht'likh
Redenquelle	ray'den-kvel'eh
Religionsgeschichte	ray'lig-ee-ohns'ge-shikh'teh
religionsgeschichtlich	ray'lig-ee-ohns'ge-shikht'likh

---

a cat, ah father, ahr lard, air care, aw jaw, ay pay, b bug, ch chew, d do,
e, eh pet, ee seem, er error, f fun, g good, h hot, hw whether, i it, *i* sky,
ihr ear, j joke, k king, kh ch as in German *Buch*, ks vex, kw quill, l love, m mat,

Religionsgeschichtliche Schule	ray'lig-ee-ohns'ge-shikht'likh-eh-shool'eh
Rheims	reemz
Rheims-Douay	reemz-d*oo*'ay
rib	reeb
ribh	reev
riv	reev
Rosetta	roh-zet'uh
Rosh Hashannah	rosh'huh-shah'nuh

S

Sachkritik	zahkh'kri-teek'
Saetze heiligen Rechtes	zayt'seh-h*i*l'i-gen-rekh'tes
Sage	zah'geh
Sahidic	suh-hid'ik
sarcophagi	sahr-kof'uh-g*i*
sarcophagus	sahr-kof'uh-guhs
schism	siz'uhm
schismatic	siz-mat'ik
scholia	skoh'lee-uh
scholion	skoh'lee-uhn
sedheq	se'dek
Seleucid	si-l*oo*'sid
semiotic	sem'ee-ot'ik
Semite	sem'*i*t
Semitic	si-mit'ik
Semiticism	si-mit'uh-siz'uhm
Semitism	sem'uh-tiz'uhm
Seneca	sen'uh-kuh
sensus litteralis	sen'soos-lit'uh-rah'lis
Sepphoris	sef'uh-ris
Septuagint	sep't*oo*-uh-jint
Septuagintal	sep't*oo*-uh-jin'tuhl
Septuagintism	sep't*oo*-uh-jin-tiz'uhm
sepulcher	sep'uhl-kuhr
sepulchre	sep'uhl-kuhr
Serapis	si-rah'pis
Sextus	seks'toos
Shekinah	shuh-k*i*'nuh
Shema	shuh-mah'

---

n not, ng sing, o hot, oh go, oi boy, oo foot, *oo* boot, oor poor, or for,
ou how, p pat, r run, s so, sh sure, t toe, th thin, *th* then, ts tsetse,
tw twin, uh ago, uhr her, v vow, w weather, y young, z zone, zh vision

shofar	shoh'fahr
shophar	shoh'fahr
Sibylline	sib'uh-leen
Sicarii	si-kahr'ee-*i*
Sicarius	si-kahr'ee-oos
sich realisierende Eschatologie	zikh-ray'-ah-li-zee'ren-deh-es'khah-toh-loh'gee
simile	sim'uh-lee
similitude	si-mil'uh-ty*oo*d
Sinaitic	s*i*n'i-it'ik
Sinaiticus	s*i*n'i-it'uh-kuhs
Sitz im Leben	zits'im-lay'buhn
Skythopolis	ski-thop'uh-lis
Slavonic	sluh-von'ik
Smyrnaean	smuhr'nee-uhn
Solomonic	sol'uh-mon'ik
Sondergut	zon'der-g*oo*t
Sopherim	soh'fuh-rim
Sophia	soh-fee'uh
soteriological	soh-tihr'ee-uh-loj'i-kuhl
soteriology	soh-tihr'ee-ol'uh-jee
Spaet-Judentum	shpayt'y*oo*-den'toom
Sprachereignis	shprahkh'er-*i*g'nis
stela	stee'luh
stelae	stee'lee
stele	stee'lee
stoa	stoh'uh
Stoicism	stoh'i-siz'uhm
Strabo	stray'boh
Streitgespraech	shtr*i*t'ge-shpraykh
strophe	stroh'fee
Suetonius	swi-toh'nee-uhs
sui ipsius interpres	s*oo*'ee-ip'see-oos-in-ter'prays
Sumer	s*oo*'muhr
Sumeria	s*oo*-maihr'ee-uh
Sumerian	s*oo*-maihr'ee-uhn
suzerain	s*oo*'zuh-ruhn
suzerainty	s*oo*'zuh-ruhn-tee
Symmachus	sim'uh-kuhs
synagogal	sin'uh-gog'uhl
synchronic	sin-kron'ik
syncretism	sin'kruh-tiz'uhm
syncretistic	sin'kruh-tis'tik
synecdoche	sin-ek'duh-kee
synopsis	sin-op'sis

a cat, ah father, ahr lard, air care, aw jaw, ay pay, b bug, ch chew, d do,
e, eh pet, ee seem, er error, f fun, g good, h hot, hw whether, i it, *i* sky,
ihr ear, j joke, k king, kh ch as in German Buch, ks vex, kw quill, l love, m mat,

synoptic	sin-op′tik
Syriac	sihr′ee-ak
Syro-Ephraimite	si′roh-ee′fray-uh-mit
Syro-Israelite	si′roh-is′ray-uh-lit

T

Tacitus	tas′uh-tuhs
Talmud	tal′mood
Talmudic	tal-mood′ik
Tanach	tah′nahk
Tanak	tah′nahk
Tanakh	tah′nahk
Targum	tahr′guhm
Targumim	tahr′guh-mim
Tatian	tay′shuhn
Taurus	taw′ruhs
tell	tel
Tell el-Amarna	tel′el-uh-mahr′nuh
Tendenz	ten-dents′
Tendenzkritik	ten-dents′kri-teek′
terminus ad quem	ter′mi-noos-ahd-kwem′
terminus a quo	ter′mi-noos-ah-kwoh′
terminus technicus	ter′mi-noos-tek′ni-koos
Tertullian	tuhr′tuhl′ee-uhn
Tetragrammaton	tet′ruh-gram′uh-ton
Tetrateuch	tet′truh-tyook
Textus Receptus	teks′tuhs-ri-sep′tuhs
Thecla	thek′luh
theios aner	thay′ohs-an-ayr′
theocracy	thee-ok′ruh-see
theocratic	thee-uh-krat′ik
theodicy	thee-od′uh-see
Theodotion	thee′uh-doh′shuhn
theological	thee′uh-loj′i-kuhl
theology	thee-ol′uh-jee
theophany	thee-of′uh-nee
theophoric	thee′uh-for′ik
Thrace	thrays
Thutmose	thyoot′mohs
Thut-mose	thyoot′mohs

n not, ng sing, o hot, oh go, oi boy, oo foot, oo boot, oor poor, or for,
ou how, p pat, r run, s so, sh sure, t toe, th thin, th then, ts tsetse,
tw twin, uh ago, uhr her, v vow, w weather, y young, z zone, zh vision

Tiamat	tee-ah'maht
Tindale	tin'duhl
Tishri	tish'ree
toparch	top'ahrk
toparchy	top'ahr-kee
Tosephta	toh-sef'tuh
Traditionsgeschichte	trah-dit'-see-ohns'ge-shikh'teh
traditionsgeschichtlich	trah-dit'see-ohns'ge-shikht'likh
Trajan	tray'juhn
Trallian	tral'yuhn
Transfiguration	trans'fig'-yuh-ray'shuhn
transfigure	trans-fig'yuhr
Trito-Isaiah	tree'toh-*i*-zay'yuh
trope	trohp
tropological	troh'puh-loj'i-kuhl
tropology	troh-pol'uh-jee
tsade	tsah'deh
Tyana	t*i*-an'uh
Tyndale	tin'duhl
typological	t*i*'puh-loj'i-kuhl
typology	t*i*-pol'uh-jee
Tyropoeon	t*i*-roh'pee-uhn

U

Ueberlieferungsgeschichte	y*oo*'ber-leef-uhr-oongs'ge-shikh-teh
ueberlieferungsgeschichtlich	y*oo*'ber-leef-uhr-oongs-ge-shikht'likh
Ugarit	*oo*'guh-rit
Ugaritic	*oo*'guh-rit'ik
uncial	un'shuhl
Ur-Evangelium	oor'i-van-jel'ee-uhm
Urgemeinde	oor'ge-m*i*n'deh
Urgeschichte	oor'ge-shikh'teh
Urkirche	oor-kihr'kheh
Ur-Marcus	oor-mahr'kuhs
Ur-Mark	oor-mahrk'
Ur-Markus	oor-mahr'kuhs
Urzeit	oor'ts*i*t

---

a cat, ah father, ahr lard, air care, aw jaw, ay pay, b bug, ch chew, d do,
e, eh pet, ee seem, er error, f fun, g good, h hot, hw whether, i it, *i* sky,
ihr ear, j joke, k king, kh ch as in German Buch, ks vex, kw quill, l love, m mat,

V

Valentinian	val'uhn-tin'ee-uhn
Valentinus	val'uhn-teen'uhs
Vaticanus	vat'i-kan'uhs
vaticinium ex eventu	wah-ti-kin'ee-oom-eks-eh-wen't*oo*
Veadar	vay'ah-dahr
vellum	vel'uhm
Veronica	vuh-ron'i-kuh
Vespasian	ves-pay'zhuhn
Via Appia	wee'ah-ah'pee-uh
Via Dolorosa	vee'uh-doh-luh-roh'suh
Via Egnatia	vee'uh-eg-nah'tee-uh
Volksspruch	fohlks'shprookh
Vorlage	fohr'lah-geh
Vulgate	vuhl'gayt

W

Wyclif	wik'lif
Wycliffe	wik'lif

Y

Yahveh	yah'weh
Yahvist	yah'wist
Yahwist	yah'wist
Yam Suph	yahm-s*oo*f'
yarmulke	yah'muhl-kuh
Yom Kippur	yom'kip'uhr

---

n not, ng sing, o hot, oh go, oi boy, oo foot, *oo* boot, oor poor, or for,
ou how, p pat, r run, s so, sh sure, t toe, th thin, *th* then, ts tsetse,
tw twin, uh ago, uhr her, v vow, w weather, y young, z zone, zh vision

Z

Zarathushtra	zair'uh-th*oo*sh'truh
Zarathustra	zair'uh-th*oo*s'truh
Zealotism	zel'uht-iz'uhm
ziggurat	zig'oo-rat
Zoroaster	zoh'roh-as'tuhr
Zoroastrian	zoh'roh-as'tree-uhn
Zoroastrianism	zoh'roh-as'tree-uhn-iz'uhm
Zostrianos	zohs'tree-ah'nohs
Zostrianus	zohs'tree-ah'nuhs